Hontology

Depressive Anthropology and the Shame of Life

Mark Payne

zero
books

Winchester, UK
Washington, USA

First published by Zero Books, 2018
Zero Books is an imprint of John Hunt Publishing Ltd., Laurel House, Station Approach,
Alresford, Hants, SO24 9JH, UK
office1@jhpbooks.net
www.johnhuntpublishing.com
www.zero-books.net

For distributor details and how to order please visit the 'Ordering' section on our website.

Text copyright: Mark Payne 2017

ISBN: 978 1 78535 731 2
978 1 78535 732 9 (ebook)
Library of Congress Control Number: 2017938670

A CIP catalogue record for this book is available from the British Library.

Design: Stuart Davies

Printed and bound by CPI Group (UK) Ltd, Croydon, CR0 4YY, UK

We operate a distinctive and ethical publishing philosophy in
all areas of our business, from our global network of authors to
production and worldwide distribution.

Contents

Acknowledgments

This book owes its slow, painful emergence into the light of day to protracted conversations with students past and present at the University of Chicago. If you don't like it, you should blame them for encouraging me. Their names are: Scott Bear Don't Walk, Ben Jeffery, Patrick Morrissey, Julia Mueller, Luke Parker, and Alba Tomasula y Garcia. My previous books are *Theocritus and the Invention of Fiction* (Cambridge University Press, 2007) and *The Animal Part: Human and Other Animals in the Poetic Imagination* (The University of Chicago Press, 2010).

1

The shame of life

Derrida's *Specters of Marx* has had an enormous influence on recent thought about the fate of human capabilities in late capitalism, especially in Europe — I am thinking, of course, of the late Mark Fisher, and of *Ghosts of My Life*, in particular. What I want to do in this book is to explore a road not taken in *Specters of Marx* — the idea that shame is the route by which we access the capabilities for living that are abrogated in modernity. This is the hontology of my title, as opposed to the hauntology that Fisher took up. More particularly still, I want to consider the loss of the New World as a horizon in which these abrogated capabilities were still in play, and the inhabitants of the New World as presenting forms of life before which Europeans felt shame in comparison with their own. Finally, I want to think — quite speculatively — about what might take the place of the New World now that its productive horizon of shame has receded from view.

Shame — *la honte* — makes its only appearance in *Specters of Marx* as a prelude to the conjuration of Marx:

> More than a year ago, I had chosen to name the "specters" by their name starting with the title of this opening lecture. "Specters of Marx," the common noun and the proper name had thus been printed, they were already on the poster when, very recently, I reread *The Manifesto of the Communist Party*. I confess it to my shame: I had not done so for decades — and that must tell one something. I knew very well there was a ghost waiting there, and from the opening, from the raising of the curtain. Now, of course, I have just discovered, in truth I have just remembered what must have been haunting my

1

memory: the *first noun* of the *Manifesto*, and this time in the singular, is "specter": "A specter is haunting Europe — the specter of communism."

What is this specter-ridden Europe? Or, more to the point, where is it? Derrida will go on to imagine that if Marx had gotten some help with the *Manifesto*, "he would have diagnosed today the same conjuration, this time not only in old Europe, but in the new Europe, the New World, which had already interested him very much a century and a half ago..." Derrida updates his specters to the geopolitical realities of the present, most obviously the hegemony of the United States, but at what cost? What disappears in this remarkable apposition, "the new Europe, the New World," is the possibility that the New World might have been — might even still be — something other than the new Europe. More precisely, it is the possibility that the New World, in its non-Europeanness, might tell old Europe something about itself; that the oldness of the New World might show new Europe what it once was, put it in touch again with its own primordial capabilities, lost to it in the present, but reproduced — to its shame — in the spectral image of the inhabitants of the New World.

"I confess it to my shame." *Je l'avoue dans la honte.* We never hear from this shame again. We hear the interruption of ontology that hauntology stages, but we never arrive at a hontology, the ontic shame of the confessional. Let us remind ourselves that *Specters of Marx* does not begin with a conjuration of Marx, but with a question about what it would be like to be really alive in the present: "Someone, you or me, comes forward and says: *I would like to learn to live finally.*" The questioner senses that the life he is living is not really life, not all that life could or ought to be. Perhaps he is ashamed of the person he is. We can put his question on hold by turning it back on him, asking him (rhetorically) whether "to learn to live, to learn it *from oneself and by oneself,* all alone...is not impossible for a living being?" And by confirming that there can be no question of teaching ourselves how to live, we fashion an entrance for Marx and his specters — the ethics and politics that follow in his train.

But this is not what the questioner was asking about. The questioner wanted to live now, not tomorrow, and he (is it?) wanted to know what was stopping him from living — really living — in the present. He is looking for someone at the "edge of life" who can teach him how to live. This edge is not a border in time — the limit of life and death — but a border in space — the frontier (perhaps) that once separated the New World from Europe, that held them apart and prevented their being collapsed into one another in acts of breathless apposition. The questioner wants to know if there is anywhere he can look to see what life looks like when it is really being lived. He is open to the idea that there might be such a place. He never meant to suggest that learning to live meant learning *"from oneself and by oneself,* all alone." Is the other who can teach us still there? Is there any place we can catch up to him and the shame he inspires in us?

"There will never be another New World." In "A Little Glass of Rum," Claude Lévi-Strauss looks ahead to the end of anthropology, when there will no longer be any place anywhere in the world where it will be possible to witness forms of life that are meaningfully different from those in Europe. "For us European earth-dwellers," he reflects, "the adventure played out in the heart of the New World" is over. All that remains is responsibility for the crime of its destruction, and a lingering awareness that the opportunity to become conscious of ourselves that the confrontation with the New World offered is now gone.

For Lévi-Strauss, it was Rousseau who best understood what was at stake in this missed opportunity. In the superior capabilities of the inhabitants of the New World Rousseau saw everything that Europeans were incapable of in their over-developed forms of social organization reflected back to him as losses — powers for the living of a genuinely happy life that Europeans had surrendered, and then forgotten they ever had. Foremost among these is the opportunity to live life in the pursuit of matters of life and death — what, in *The Discourse on the Arts and Sciences*, he calls "duties and natural needs," in contrast to the "barren thoughts" that are the content of a civilized person's existence, and which represent an effort to distract ourselves from the melancholy that infects our lives when the pursuit of natural goals recedes from the horizon of individual achievement. Second is the contentment in the sensation of existence that suffuses a person's life when it is lived in the pursuit of these goals. Whereas Europeans have outsourced the feeling of their own existence to the judgment of others, because they only live in the opinion of others, the inhabitants of the New World live within themselves. The sentiment of their own existence fills their lives and gives them a tranquility that, in *The Discourse on Inequality*, Rousseau compares to the ataraxia, or freedom from care, of the ancient Stoics.

As Lévi-Strauss understands perfectly, the age to which Rousseau cathects is a speculative Neolithic, a period in human development at which certain thresholds of security have been attained with regard to cold, hunger, and rest, but without the hypertrophic development of social life by which he felt himself shorn of his own best capabilities as a human animal. Lévi-Strauss also understands perfectly that this cathexis is an obligatory method for Rousseau. We must attend to the times and places on which we are inclined to fixate because the obsessiveness of our recursive attention points to a defect, or insufficiency, in ourselves that we would not otherwise discover:

There is, I sense, an age at which the individual human being would want to stop; you will look for the age at which you would wish your species had stopped. Discontented with

4

your present state, for reasons that herald even greater discontents for your unhappy posterity, you might perhaps wish to be able to go backwards.

Rousseau's depressive anthropology is a speculative project, but a speculative project that is provoked by concrete examples. Without the encounter with the New World and its inhabitants, European theorists would never have thought to interrogate their own form of life as a loss of powers, but this consideration of loss has to be the starting point for any kind of social critique. It is only by understanding what we miss that we can know what to aim for, and it is only by looking inside after first looking outside that we can know what we miss. By showing that the state of nature, "which no longer exists, which perhaps never existed, and which will probably never exist in the future," is nonetheless the very thing of which it is essential to have a sound conception in order to pass valid judgment on the present, it was Rousseau, "our master and brother," Lévi-Strauss claims, who taught us that, "after demolishing all forms of social organization, we can still discover the principles which will allow us to construct a new form."

It is this belief that takes Lévi-Strauss to South America to meet the Nambikwara and other Amazonian peoples. It is only in the encounter with concrete possibilities that the shamed self of European social life can acknowledge its desire for a fuller existence than it is presently capable of and recognize what is denied to it in its present state of incapacity. Lévi-Strauss rues the imminent loss of the possibility for a face-to-face encounter with this horizon of human capabilities. For Lévi-Strauss, as for Rousseau, this loss brings the potential for a total social "enslavement" into view, when there will no longer be any possibility of formulating speculative alternatives to the ontic shame in which the anthropological project originates:

Western Europe may have produced anthropologists precisely because it was a prey to strong feelings of remorse, which forced it to compare its image with those of different societies in the hope that they would show the same defects or would help to explain how its own defects had developed within it...The anthropologist is the less able to ignore his own civilization and to dissociate himself from its faults in that his very existence is incomprehensible except as an attempt at redemption: he is the symbol of atonement.

Lévi-Strauss's language of defect looks back to Rousseau's point of departure in *The Discourse on Inequality*, which begins with an epigraph from Aristotle's *Politics*: "What is natural has to be investigated not in beings that are depraved, but in those that are good according to nature." For Aristotle, this investigation does not entail probing the dim reaches of the past, or trying to grasp what is barely known about other places and other times, as it does for Rousseau. For Aristotle, it is only by living in cities that human beings are able to realize the potential that is naturally theirs as human beings. Cities are ontologically prior to singular human beings, for it is only in cities that there is really such a thing as a human being whose limits and capabilities can be thought about. There could be no sense and no value in a project such as Rousseau's, which seeks to discover what social life has taken away from human beings through speculative reflection on a distant pre-social other. Human beings at lower levels of social organization are either wild animals or gods, and so do not belong to the study of the *anthropos* at all.

For Aristotle, human beings lend themselves to understanding, because they are everywhere present in the form of life that best allows them to be understood. Social form and cognitive ambition dovetail perfectly. For Rousseau, by contrast, having a cognitive ambition may be the very thing that makes its realization impossible, and the contrast with Aristotle that his epigraph points to seems designed to focus attention on the difficulty of the speculative task he has set himself: "It is by dint of studying man that we have made it impossible to know him." There can be no question of identifying human possibilities with "the men we have before our eyes," as Aristotle does.

Rousseau frets about the limitations of his anthropological materials, and worries that his European informants see only themselves in the non-European people they encounter. The closer you get to the object that troubles complacent resignation to your own form of life, the more effectively the mechanisms of repression kick in that prevent you from seeing it for what it really is. But the speculative subject finds a way out of this impasse by recognizing its abrogated pleasure in the sentiment of its own existence amplified in its non-Western reflection. Speculation is fueled by a primordial relation to this denied sense of life that allows it to see beyond its shame.

What Rousseau practices is introspection in the person of the other. This second person introspection internalizes the dialogue with the native informant that was popularized in France by Baron Lahontan's fictive dialogue with the Huron chief Adario. One might think that Rousseau's internalization of the dialogue is an occlusion or erasure of the other who provokes reflective introspection, and that the force of the encounter would have its greatest impact in a fully imagined and externalized dialogue like that of Lahontan. But Rousseau's method is grounded in his doubt about the viability of his cognitive project, and the slim hope it affords of recovering a feeling for his speculative Neolithic as it is encountered in the figure of the New World inhabitant, who, unlike the European earth-dweller, is still "carrying all of himself along with him." In Lahontan, this possibility is abjected on to the other for contemplation, whereas Rousseau is already so anxious about the outsourcing of capabilities that he prefers to feel his way towards their recovery and reincorporation through introspective uptake of the other as a lost or ghost self within.

Rousseau's is in every sense a depressive anthropology — beginning in shame, mistrustful of its methods and materials, and dubious about its own chances of success. Yet, as New World inhabitants have not been slow to recognize, it is when anthropology loses touch with its depressive origins that it substitutes descriptive fullness for self-interrogation, and produces simulations instead of insight. In *Manifest Manners*, Gerald Vizenor points to the indispensable link between Western melancholy and New World anthropology. The "inventions of tribal cultures" can be traced to "the truancies and cruelties of a melancholy civilization" whose front line agents are missionaries and ethnologists. It is Vizenor's understanding that melancholy informs this ethnographic project in an occluded, frustrated form that leads him to place so much emphasis on the trickster as an anti-melancholic performative individual who works to undo the totalizing construction of culture by the ethnographic subject who has lost touch with the depressive origins of his project:

> Native American Indian imagination and the pleasures of language games are disheartened in the manifest manners of documentation and the imposition of cultural representation; tribal testimonies are unheard, and tricksters, the wild ironies of survivance, transformation, natural reason, and liberation in stories, are marooned as obscure moral simulations in translations.

"Colonial historicism," as Vizenor calls cultural poetics, is the production of obscure moral simulations by a melancholy civilization that, in ways that are now unknown to itself, is chasing its own lost powers in its meticulous ethnographies of Indian life. Survivance is the opposite of the "thick description" that readers of ethnography are accustomed to praise as it moves them from melancholy self-attention towards the work of mourning and moving on. Survivance consists of thin gestures at what could actually be lived, or has actually been lived, in the present or the past, that do not entrap tribal survivors in the repetition of a cultural simulation.

Survivance, ethnographic simulation, and depressive anthropology alike are often enacted along the axis of connectivity to living beings as a whole, for it is here that the sentiment of life is most fully in play as an occasion for liberation in stories, for cultural representation, and for melancholic regret respectively. Each of them can be analyzed at work in D'Arcy McNickle's *The Surrounded*.

McNickle's novel investigates the psychic consequences of the transition to reservation life on the Salish (Flathead) Reservation in western Montana. Archilde Leon returns to the reservation from Portland where he has been working as a musician to stay with his Spanish father and Indian mother. Archilde accompanies his mother on a late fall hunting trip to the mountains, where they are joined by Archilde's brother. A game warden shows up at their camp and questions their right to hunt, and in the ensuing standoff, the game warden kills Archilde's brother, and Archilde's mother kills the game warden. The killings remain undiscovered during the winter months, and in this time Archilde becomes reconciled to the traditionalism of the elders of his tribe. In spring, however, the local sheriff takes the search for the game warden's body in hand, and Archilde, his girlfriend, Elise, and two of his nephews take off for the mountains, where they are quickly discovered. Elise kills the sheriff, but she and Archilde are captured by the reservation agent and an Indian policeman, who have accompanied the sheriff as backup. The nephews ride off, deeper into the mountains.

What coming to terms with reservation life means for Archilde is finding a way forward from fixation on a past life that was meaningful because it had the satisfaction of natural needs continuously in view towards survivance as the effort to preserve a living memory of such a life as something other than a culturalist simulation. When Archilde sets off on his hunting trip with his mother, he has a fleeting sense of the identity of their present actions with the historical life of the tribe. His own moving through the landscape seems to be overlaid directly on to the living presence of the past: "This was how it would have seemed years ago, crossing the mountains to hunt buffalo. Nothing would have been much different." But as he reflects on why he and his mother are going, this sense of continuous life is evacuated from his surroundings and he is left with a feeling of lifeless repetition instead:

> But it was different. The mountains were empty of life, that was the difference. This ride with his mother was no more than a pleasure trip; that was the difference. If they returned without fresh meat, no one would worry; at home there were canned peas, potatoes in the cellar, and meat could be had at the butcher's; that was the difference.

The historical form of life of the Salish was more real than their present life. Every action in it could immediately be understood as worth doing because it was grounded in the close presence of life and death for the tribe as a whole, in their shared life with one another, with other tribes, and with the plants and animals on which their survival depended. As his uncle, Modeste, sums it up for Archilde, in the present "you will die easily, but if you had lived then you might have died fighting to live." It makes no difference now whether they hunt or don't hunt. However much game they kill, the mountains are "empty of life." Hunting is now just a form of recreational tourism, and there is no point in shooting a deer just because you can.

Archilde's melancholy originates in his inability to feel in the present the primordial satisfaction of action for the sake of life. He does not fully understand his own melancholy because he is shut out from its causes and, as a result, he also cannot initially understand the commitment on the part of the old people of his tribe to perpetuating the memory of their historical form of life. He views it as a derealization of the present for the sake of a simulation of the past that has passed them by. He is unable to access his own melancholy and abjects it on to them. He thinks the past has usurped their present, so as to foreclose their being present to themselves, but his understanding of the situation changes when Modeste tells a story that allows Archilde to see for himself why this life was in fact more real than the life they live now, and not just for them:

> For the first time he had really seen it happen. First the great numbers and the power, then the falling away, the battles and the starvation in the snow, the new hopes and the slow facing of disappointment, and then no hope at all, just this living in the past. He had heard the story many times, but he had not listened. It had tired him. Now he saw that it had happened and it left him feeling weak. It destroyed his stiffness toward the old people. He sat and thought about it and the flames shot upward and made light on the circle of black pines.

Archilde comes to introspection in the person of the other and thereby accepts survivance as care for a historical form of life. Acceptance makes it possible for him to recover a shared life in the present that is grounded in this care. He looks after his relatives when they come to his house after his mother's death, and he looks out for his young nephews during their flight to the mountains. With the discovery of care, Archilde discovers that "he too belonged to the story of *Sniél-emen*," the mountains of the surrounded, as they are called in the novel's epigraph. But Archilde belongs to *Sniél-emen* tragically. His retreat with Elise and his nephews into a "high, snug canyon" in the mountains — the valley of the Salish in miniature — is cut short by the appearance of Quigley, the sheriff, and, in his train, the reservation agent and the Indian policeman. The apprehension of a pre-Christian, pre-reservation shared life that guided him to the mountains will not perdure without a grounding in material existence that he cannot provide, and he is forced to acknowledge a truth that his nephews had seen more clearly than he had in the eyes of the priest who taught them "how much greater — how everlasting — was the world of priests and schools, the world which engulfed them."

Archilde does not misunderstand survivance as a commitment to enact a historical form of life when it is impossible to do so in the present. His fate is tragic because he is haunted by an action that precedes his understanding of survivance, and cuts short his ability to perpetuate it non-tragically. Relations with animals figure Archilde's transition from melancholic self-occlusion to a mature understanding of the ethics of survivance. At the outset of *The Surrounded*, Archilde identifies his tribe's relictualized form of life with the small herd of buffalo that is co-located with them, behind the wire enclosure of a Biological Survey. His uncle and his mother "were not real people," just as "buffaloes were not real to him either," since they too now live in a reserve instead of moving freely through their world. The buffaloes "had been real things to his mother, and to the old people," but they, like the old people themselves, have now been absorbed into the fantasmatic life of the past. Later, however, when Archilde withdraws temporarily into the badlands on the edge of the reservation to reflect on his experience since his return, he finds a half-starved mare with her foal, and attempts to rescue her against her will. He ropes her and leads her back to his camp, where she dies:

In the end he wore her down. And when finally she stopped, with quivering legs braced and her eyes glaring, the anger and will to overcome which the chase had aroused in him collapsed. He was left limp and ashamed…She groaned aloud, a final note of reproach for the ears of the man who had taken it upon himself to improve her condition.

Whereas Archilde cannot cathect to the derealized, hyper-real buffalo, the horses allow an understanding of his situation in relation to his people to emerge. Because they refuse his efforts to improve them, they allow for care instead, as the feeling for what remains, a feeling that only emerges after the initial rage that expresses itself as violent-care — care against their will — is spent. A version of this scene recurs in James Welch's *Winter in the Blood*. The novella is set on the Fort Belknap reservation in northern Montana, and its unnamed narrator's efforts to feel at home there culminate in an apprehension of shared life with his horse in the common harm that has been done to both of them alike:

A cow horse. You weren't born that way; you were born to eat your grass and drink slough water, to nip the other horses in the flanks the way you do the lagging bulls, to mount the mares. So they cut off your balls to make you less temperamental, though I think they failed at that. They haltered you, blindfolded you, waved gunnysacks at you and slapped you across the neck, the back with leather. Finally they saddled you — didn't you try to kick them when they reached under your belly for the cinch? — and a man climbed on you for the first time. Only you can tell me how it felt to stand quivering under the weight of that first man, dumbfounded until — was it? — panic and anger began to spread through your muscles and you erupted, rearing, lunging, sunfishing around the corral until the man had dug a furrow with his nose in the soft, flaky manure. You must have felt cocky, proud, but the man — who was it? — surely not First Raise — the man climbed on your back again and began to rake you with his spurs. Again you reared and threw the man; again he dusted himself off and climbed back on. Again and again, until you were only crowhopping and running and swerving and the man clung to the saddle horn and jerked your head first one way, then the other, until you were confused and half-blind with frustration. But you weren't through. There was the final step — turn him out, somebody said, you heard it — and you raced through the open gate, down the rutted road, your neck stretched out as though you were after a carrot, and the man's spurs dug deep in your ribs. You ran and ran for what must have seemed like miles, not always following the road, but always straight ahead, until you thought your heart would explode against the terrible constriction of its cage. It was this necessity, this knowledge of death, that made you slow down to a stiff-legged trot, bearing sideways, then a walk, and finally you found yourself standing under a hot sun in the middle of a field of foxtail and speargrass, wheezing desperately to suck in the heavy air of a summer's afternoon. Not even the whirr of a sage hen as it lifted from a clump of rosebush ten feet away could make you lift that young tired head.

A cow horse.

There is no more magical realism in *Winter in the Blood* than there is in *A Farewell to Arms*. Yet this passage is properly understood as the voice of a horse. Not the projection of a human voice into an animal but human speech made the organ of communication for another life form. The unobtrusiveness of the realist novella allows the reader to grasp the understanding between human being and horse revered in Plains culture without making it a lifeless re-performance of tradition. The protagonist's apprehension of the possibility of a single biography not just for himself and his horse, but for horses and Indians in general, has as its deep background the knowledge that the idea of a people once held for animals other than human beings. This horizon of shared life has shrunk to commonalities of suffering between singular beings, but part of the novella's staging of shared life in its tragic modality is its acknowledgment of just this limitation, and its not shrinking away from the face with which shared life does in fact draw close in the present. This is what survivance looks like. The suggestion that melancholic apprehension of shared life with beings as a whole might open up the form of the novella to a kind of story it cannot actually accommodate is a kind of trickster poetics — it makes something happen, or allows for something to happen, without explaining why it is possible.

Survivance is a way of caring for the past that provides a threshold or opening for possibility to emerge without making it into a call for the repetition of a simulation. Frank Linderman's *Pretty-shield: Medicine Woman of the Crows* has the form of Indian biography in which an indigenous person raised in pre-reservation days recounts his or her life story to a white person some years after the historical form of life it describes has come to an end. Linderman, who by the time he recorded it had spent several decades among the Crow, remarks that it was unusual to meet an older Crow woman interested in engaging in this form of reminiscence, since the genre of biography was alien to Crow culture, and especially to Crow women. Linderman also stands out among contemporary Indian biographers for the degree to which he acknowledges gaps, breaks, and reformulations in his presentation of Pretty-shield's words. Pretty-shield speaks to him in Crow via an interpreter, although they occasionally communicate directly in Plains sign language, and he is at pains to portray the full setting in which their dialogue unfolds, documenting food breaks, interruptions by grandchildren, and even the tribulations of the cabin stove by the side of which the transcription takes place.

The following episode is exemplary. Pretty-shield has just asked Linderman what he would like to hear about next, and he has replied, as he always does, that he would like to hear about the old days and her life as a girl. She responds with anecdotes about the dangers of berry picking when bears are around, then goes on to tell a couple of stories that illustrate how her own desire to make pets of baby animals almost got her into trouble when she was young. In the first, she describes a male bear cub who appeared eager to live with her after getting cuffed by his mother, and how she had to drop this "little boy-bear" who "acted exactly like a naughty Crow boy" when the "woman-bear," its mother, started in pursuit of them. After an interruption from Pretty-shield's grandchildren, the narrative resumes with a story about kidnapping antelope. While out digging for edible roots, Pretty-shield and her friends once came upon a pair of young antelope asleep on a rock ledge in the sun and decided to take them home as pets. The babies cry out as their legs are tied and their mother duly appears in response to their cries:

"Suddenly, as though some medicine had told her what to do, she ran to the ledge of the rock, and began to beat it with her hoofs, as though beating a drum. And then she began to sing, keeping time on the rock with her hoofs. I understood her words."

Reaching for one of my pencils, Pretty-shield stood up and with it began to drum on the table-top, her intelligent face almost fanatical. "Tap-tap — tap-tap — tap-tap — tap-tap." And then she sang:

"'Who is going to have the smartest children?

The one that has the straight ears.

Get up and run; run on.'

She sang this song four times," she said, sitting down again, the pencil yet in her hand. "I could not stand it to hear her, a mother, sing that way. I thought of how my own heart would feel if somebody stole children that belonged to me. I untied my baby antelope. 'Go,' I told it, feeling glad to see it run to its mother."

Pretty-shield ends her story by saying that her companions released the other baby antelope and that the mother antelope's song has never left her. In fact, she sings its song to her grandchildren when they are fretful at night, and when she does so, as she did the previous evening, they always go right to sleep. Finally, she reflects "mistily" that, "the antelope are a strange people," since, while they are beautiful to look at, they are also tricky, and so the Crow do not trust them: "They appear and disappear; they are like shadows on the plain." Because of the beauty of the antelope, she adds, young men sometimes follow them and are lost. If they eventually find their way home, they are "never again right in their heads." Such strangeness "has always belonged to the antelope," and she tells another story to illustrate her point: Crow girls out playing ball encounter a pair of beautiful girls who, when they are seen from behind, turn out to be antelope. At this point, Linderman jumps in to explain — "The antelope, beautiful, and strangely marked is so camouflaged by nature that one has difficulty in seeing them on their native plains until they present their rumps in flight" — and so the chapter ends.

When the next chapter begins, we learn right away that Pretty-shield thinks something is amiss in her communication with Linderman. "Did any of the animal-people ever talk to you," she asks him, "abruptly, moving her chair forward, her manner confidential." In response, Linderman rationalizes once again, telling her that he has often understood what his horse or his dog wished him to know. But this is not at all what Pretty-shield means: "As though pondering, she stared at the blank wall over my head, disappointment in her eyes. 'But they *do* talk,' she said, firmly, half to herself."

The proper context of Pretty-shield's *eppur si muove*, as she rejects Linderman's theorization of her story as an example of intuition, is not just the intimate scene of her conversation with Linderman, but the larger, transhistorical audience that she avails herself of by deciding, against conventional wisdom, to entrust her experience of shared life with beings as a whole to the fate of interpretation, transcription, and publication. Pretty-shield had known Linderman for a long time by the time she came to tell him her life story, and her granddaughter has recalled the pleasure she took in conversing with him. Her performance of disappointment on this occasion ensures the success of her speech act as a transformation of trickster survivance. If she speaks "half to herself," it is because she is aware that such a bifurcation of addressees has a peculiar power of drawing attention to what is being said.

Pretty-shield knows the power of the antelope song because she speaks of its effectiveness in soothing her grandchildren, and she must have known what its likely effect on Linderman would be. She chooses an instance of shared life that she knows will produce puzzlement, and ensures that its relay will be as striking as possible by not just narrating it, but actually singing it. This is the one and only time in her entire narration that she sings, and she returns to the story on the following day to further exacerbate her interlocutor's incomprehension.

Pretty-shield frequently expresses concern about what the life of the children around her will be like in years to come, and she grasps the possibilities for the transmediation of shared life in autobiography adroitly, undaunted by anxieties about linguistic and textual interference, despite all the stages of the relay involved in the transmission of the voice of the antelope to her interpreter, her biographer, and her readers. She operationalizes the communicative modalities of the relic as a figure of possibility, against the destructive derealization of self-experience in the present. She invites the transmission of her experience of shared life with beings as a whole in the unfamiliar form of autobiography and makes her antelope song at home in it. The embedded event is alien to the accommodating form, and the framing narration channels the cognitive dissonance that ensues as interpellation. Pretty-shield's challenge to Linderman's rationalization of her story relays her self-experience to the reader not as an idea about the past, but as a life actually lived. Cognitive dissonance points to a threshold of possibility that remains unexplained, and therefore capable of being taken up again in the future.

Rousseau would be the first to acknowledge that the affective horizon of ethnographic writing is fundamental to its production of knowledge. A depressive anthropologist is not simply an investigator disheartened by the abrogation of human capabilities in the present and led to introspective outlining of a historical form of life as its alternative. An exorbitant idea of life looms over the present as what lived experience in the present can never reach. Hurt feelings are also part of this complex, for modern social life puts the judgment of others in place of the pleasure we ought to feel in our own being. The modern European derives the sentiment of his own existence *solely* from the judgment of others, and the zero sum game of feeling played out between the judgment of others and the sentiment of life structures Rousseau's speculative reconstruction of human history, from the humiliating comparison of his own age with the ancient Spartans in the *Discourse on the Arts and Sciences*, to the claim in *The Discourse on Inequality* that "man's first sentiment was that of his existence," and the discovery in the *Reveries* that withdrawal from social life allows an efflorescence of this feeling in ways he would not have previously thought possible.

In *The Discourse on Inequality*, this feeling remains at the very horizon of the possibilities that Rousseau is trying to reach through his depressive anthropology: "How are we to imagine the sort of pleasure that a savage takes in spending his life alone in the depths of forests, or fishing, or blowing into a poor flute without ever managing to draw a single note from it and without troubling to learn to do so?" But in the second *Reverie*, he recalls being run over by a carriage in Paris, and his surprise on returning to consciousness at just how capacious and extensive the feeling for life can be:

> Night was coming on. I saw the sky, some stars, and a few leaves. This first sensation was a moment of delight. I was conscious of nothing else. In this instant I was being born again, and it seemed as if all I perceived was filled with my frail existence. Entirely taken up by the present, I could remember nothing; I had no distinct notion of myself as a person, nor had I the least idea of what had just happened to me. I did not know who I was, nor where I was; I felt neither pain, fear, nor anxiety. I watched my blood flowing as I might have watched a stream, without even thinking that the blood had anything to do with me. I felt throughout my whole being such a wonderful calm, that whenever I recall this feeling I can find nothing to compare with it in all the pleasures that stir our lives.

Traumatic identification with the universe as a whole is a limit experience, but it is also the ataraxia of the ancient sages that he identified with savage tranquility. It is a token of the active relationship between self-loss and the feeling of existence that he achieved in his daily walks. In his island life on Lake Bienne, he becomes autarkic — "self-sufficient like God" — as he grows accustomed to the satisfaction of natural needs and the contemplative platform this limitation affords:

> The feeling of existence unmixed with any other emotion is in itself a precious feeling of peace and contentment which would be enough to make this mode of being loved and

cherished by anyone who could guard against all the earthly and sensual influences that are constantly distracting us from it in this life and troubling the joy it could give us.

Autarky and connectivity are a positive feedback loop because self-sufficiency allows the self that has outsourced its feeling of life to the judgment of other human beings to reconnect with living beings as a whole. Depressive anthropology is enacted along this axis of connectivity to living beings as a whole, for it is here that the abrogation of the sentiment of life in the present is most fully in play as an occasion for melancholic regret and the hope of reattunement to a life gone by.

This ecstatic experience also structures historical ecology's relationship with life forms of the past. In *A Sand County Almanac*, Aldo Leopold reflects on the sandhill crane as a relic "of the remote Eocene":

> The other members of the fauna in which [the crane] originated are long since entombed within the hills. When we hear his call we hear no mere bird. We hear the trumpet in the orchestra of evolution. He is the symbol of our untamable past, of that incredible sweep of millennia which underlies and conditions the daily affairs of birds and men. And so they live and have their being — these cranes — not in the constricted present, but in the wider reaches of evolutionary time.

Evolutionary history is a channel on which human beings view their own deep historicity. The crane as relic, as spectral body in the shared life of the present, affords the opportunity for an intimate encounter with this historicity. To hear the crane on this channel is to encounter the relic in its abiding, its perduring. It is passing us by on its journey through time as it has passed others by before us, and this is why the relic is always a figure of possibility, as well as an instantiation of loss. The relic populates our world with ghostly invitations to other ways of being together, other forms of shared life. On this channel, we see other human beings living differently with cranes, with different desires for the birds and for themselves, and their ghostly appearance invites specters of the future: other human beings who might live differently with them once again.

The relic invites us to consider the kinds of self-experience that were possible alongside it once upon a time, but are disenacted in the present, and so provokes intimate reflections on the relative desirability of possible forms of life. The special appeal of the relic emerges from the relationship between intimacy and isolation in the way that it interpellates us with these possibilities for relationality. It gives us to feel the insufficiency of our present form of life for the human organism in general as a call to the singular instance of this organism that we are.

Theodore Roosevelt captures the ecstatic experience of historical ecology as the ghostly revenance of the book of life:

> I do not understand how any man or woman who really loves nature can fail to try to exert all influence in support of such objects as those of the Audubon Society. Spring would not be spring without bird songs, any more than it would be spring without buds and flowers, and I only wish that besides protecting the songsters, the birds of the grove, the orchard, the garden and the meadow, we could also protect the birds of the sea-shore and of the wilderness...How immensely it would add to our forests if the great Logcock were still found among them! The destruction of the Wild Pigeon and the Carolina Paroquet has meant a loss as severe as if the Catskills or the Palisades were taken away. When I hear of the destruction of a species I feel just as if the works of some great writer had perished; as if we had lost all instead of only

part of Polybius or Livy.

Sitting in a library, standing in a gallery, wading through a crane marsh, we are moving through a ruin. Our ordinary life world is the ruin of that other, more real, more life-like life world to which the relic invites us. The book of life is the book of life only insofar as it is also the book of death, a palimpsest underwritten by its erasures and spoilage.

Historical ecology is still subject to this haunting by vanished life. Paul Martin begins *Twilight of the Mammoths* with an epigraph from Thoreau's journal in which he expresses his "chagrin" at the loss of "primitive nature" that resulted from white settlers' extermination of the wild animals of New England. As Thoreau felt like he was living in a world that had been "maimed," "tamed," and "emasculated" by his countrymen, so Martin feels that we live in a world blighted by the extinction of the Pleistocene megafauna that disappeared 10,000 years ago, and argues that it is the loss of these animals from the "Quaternary zoo" that is the cause of the widespread indifference to contemporary extinctions:

> The absence of mammoths, ground sloths, and others derailed a much more intense involvement with American wildlife than could be developed with the blighted survivors of near-time extinctions. Most of us are more susceptible to large, warm-blooded, furry, bright-eyed mammals than to reptiles, amphibians, insects, birds, or tiny mammals such as shrews. Perhaps it is because the large mammals seem to be the most like us.

Our horizon of shared life has contracted because of these prehistoric extinctions, and the ensuing loneliness leads Martin to advocate for rewilding and resurrection ecology alike. The federal government should let wild donkeys roam freely on public lands because they are akin to extinct American equids, and it should supplement these de-domesticated European transplants with Asian and African elephants, black and white rhinoceros, oryx, and other such Old World survivals.

Martin's proposal to compensate for the Pleistocene extinctions with "Quaternary parks" has something in common with the designer ecosystems of large animals envisaged by Lee Silver, which might even include genetically engineered mythological beings like centaurs, in which friendliness to human beings has been hardwired, and even with the genomic transmediation projects of Eduardo Kac, whose "Natural History of the Enigma" is a hybrid of the petunia and the artist himself — a flower that expresses his DNA in its red veins, and is intended to instill a new sense of wonder about life by pushing public recognition of shared life beyond complacent acknowledgment of our fellow feeling with other large mammals with whom we can communicate without difficulty. In its very opposition to the complacency of the fellow feeling that lies behind Martin's proposal, Kac's project reflects a similar belief that our shared life with living beings as a whole is impoverished in the present, and must be quantitatively supplemented in order to return to us the wonder, the companionability, and even the "soulfulness" of a form of life that should rightfully be ours.

At the opposite pole to these instances of technophilic faith in a future to come is Theodore Kaczynski's recovery of depressive anthropology as a practical endeavor that keeps natural needs always in mind as the horizon of a meaningful human life. Much of what Kaczynski has to say in this regard is unoriginal, and lack of concern for his own originality is one marker of his distance from academic argument. He is unabashed about acknowledging commonalities of thought with Jacques Ellul, for example, and claims only to have given difficult and unpalatable ideas a clearer and more accessible articulation than they would otherwise have received.

Kaczynski seems to consider his most cogent contribution to the critique of technological civilization to be the practical knowledge he derived from his experience of non-social life — how much time it takes to collect firewood, prepare roots, or tan skins, for example — which allows him to articulate a more precise version of the speculative Neolithic than green anarchists who champion Marshall Sahlins' idea of Stone Age affluence, without understanding that preparation time has to be added to time spent in hunting and gathering, and that in pre-modern societies much of this painful and laborious work of survival was done by women. But when he is less occupied with critique, and has space to reflect on the satisfactions of the mountain life that he enjoyed in Montana, Kaczynski is a joyous thinker, and his pleasures are of a piece with Rousseau's sentiment of existence:

> In my life in the woods I found certain satisfactions that I had expected, such as personal freedom, independence, a certain element of adventure, and a low-stress way of life. I also achieved certain satisfactions that I hadn't fully understood or anticipated, or that even came as a complete surprise to me. The more intimate you become with nature, the more you appreciate its beauty. It's a beauty that consists not only in sights and sounds but in an appreciation of...the whole thing. I don't know how to express it. What is significant is that when you live in the woods, rather than just visiting them, the beauty becomes part of your life rather than something you just look at from the outside...
>
> In living close to nature, one discovers that happiness does not consist in maximizing pleasure. It consists in tranquility. Once you have enjoyed tranquility long enough, you acquire actually an aversion to the thought of any very strong pleasure — excessive pleasure would disrupt your tranquility...
>
> Boredom is almost nonexistent once you've become adapted to life in the woods. If you don't have any work that

needs to be done, you can sit for hours at a time just doing nothing, just listening to the birds or the wind or the silence, watching the shadows move as the sun travels, or simply looking at familiar objects. And you don't get bored. You're just at peace.

Kaczynski includes among his fondest memories of his life in the woods "certain places where I camped out during spring, summer, or autumn," and what he describes surely lies at the core of what any backpacker is seeking in a trip to the backcountry. Camp at the end of a long day's hike brings into range of feeling the outermost layer of the peaceful pleasure Kaczynski remembers here, and is a starting point for the introspective recovery of possibilities that links Kaczynski and Rousseau across time and place.

Kaczynski refers to the historiography of white flight from the settlements to the Indians in early America and he draws a similar conclusion to the one that spurred Rousseau's choice of frontispiece for *The Discourse on Inequality*. Likewise, the sense of continuous existence — of shared life with living beings as a whole — and the fading of the fear of death that comes with it is exactly the tranquility of the ancient sages that Rousseau recalls in his comparison of Stoic ataraxia to the tranquility of the Caribbean Indians. Kaczynski was a professor of mathematics at UC Berkeley, and his memoirs have a place alongside those of John Tanner in *The Falcon*, as the first hand knowledge gleaned from acting on the desire to take back the "serious, practical, purposeful, life-and-death aspects" of life into one's hands, instead of allowing them to be outsourced in the division of labor, and accepting the surrogate satisfactions of the arts and sciences in their place.

2

Greeks, Indians, and the weird tale

Depressive anthropology is enacted along the axis of connectivity to living beings as a whole, for it is here that the abrogation of the sentiment of life is most fully in play as an occasion for melancholic regret and the hope of reattunement. At a certain point on this axis we find mythology. Resurrection ecology's will to reproduce centaurs alongside the mammoth and the passenger pigeon reflects mythology's exorbitant demand for a life that is larger than the life we live. The West is haunted by the fullness of a life gone by and mythology's claim is to be a transmediation of this life, a perpetuation of what has been lived in another form. Nothing is lost for mythology. Its hyperreality is the opposite of caring for what is actually here — what is and can be lived as survivance.

It is along this axis that Greeks and Indians meet. The sadness that begins in America creeps back to Europe as a demand for more life, another life. Tocqueville remarks on the unexpected melancholy of the Americans. Indians are the source of life. All the while there are Indians, humanity hemorrhages away from the settlements, back into the forests. Benjamin Franklin fears the American experiment won't last. On the other side of the river there is an escape from the shame of life. The boy John Tanner has himself captured by the Shawnee and is sold upstream to the Ojibwe. He becomes Shaw-shaw-wa ne-ba-se, The Falcon. As he relates in *The Falcon*, this is finally a life worth living.

The invention of the Indian is the needy fabrication of a melancholy civilization. It is coeval with the invention of the Greeks and by no means a highbrow phenomenon. Gerald Vizenor's citation of Frederick Manfred's *Scarlet Plume* points to the identity of the Greek and the Indian in hyperreal simulations of an alternative to the shame of life: "He was all man. A god among men. He made her think of the old Greek heroes: Achilles and Ajax and Odysseus. She found it difficult to think him a deadly enemy, a Cuthead Sioux."

The more reflective among the inventors of the Greeks also key their inventions to the invention of the Indian so that the doubling is obvious. This gesture too originates with Rousseau. The father of depressive anthropology is also the theorist of an unspoiled Greece, inhabited by the only judges before whom he is willing to acknowledge his shame. While writing *The Discourse on Inequality*, "I shall suppose myself in the Lyceum of Athens, repeating the lesson of my masters, with the likes of Plato and Xenophanes as my judges, and mankind as my audience." This is the real mankind, as opposed to the damaged specimens to which the epigraph from Aristotle points, who would be incapable of trying the case before them. In the first *Discourse*, he calls this audience "Sparta." The frontispiece is a Greek wild man getting his beard burned off by a god inimical to humankind: Prometheus, the inventor of the sciences, and the source of the discovery that is the origin of our shame in the second *Discourse* — the appropriation of fire for human ends and the demonic arts of metallurgy.

The yearning movement towards undamaged life in the figure of the Greek and the Indian is the signature gesture of Schiller, Hölderlin, Nietzsche, and Thoreau in their invention of the past, but it has a supernatural clarity in the Anglo-American weird tale where it is enacted as the pursuit of a lost mythology whose recovery ends in death. In 1911, Algernon Blackwood published a long work of fiction about a man who discovers a lost tribe of centaurs in the Caucasus, and almost turns into one himself. H. P. Lovecraft, who considered Blackwood's "The Willows" the greatest specimen ever composed of the species of short fiction known as the weird tale, admired *The Centaur* too, but found it hard to categorize. Is it a novel? A hypertrophic story? A very long prose poem?: "Too subtle, perhaps, for definite classification as horror-tales, yet possibly more truly artistic in an absolute sense, are such delicate phantasies as *Jimbo* or *The Centaur*. Mr. Blackwood achieves in these novels a close and palpitant approach to the inmost substance of dream, and works enormous havoc with the conventional barriers between reality and imagination." In literature, just as in life, cladistical dilemmas may signal events of the greatest urgency for the pre-human, post-human, non-human thing that Blackwood calls Man.

The facts of *The Centaur* are sensational, and easily stated. An Irishman named Terence O'Malley travels to the Caucasus by ship. On board ship he is introduced to a Russian man and his son, who turn out to be centaurs traveling home in human form. O'Malley follows them to the mountains of the Caucasus, where he glimpses a herd of centaurs running wild, and very nearly becomes one himself. Blackwood develops this simple story, whose central incident — the would-be transformation — lasts only a few seconds, into a book length fable about writing and the interlinked fates of poetry, Nature, and the past at the threshold of modernity.

O'Malley is incapable of telling his own story. The novel is the first person account of an unnamed friend who inherits a sack of O'Malley's abandoned notebooks, and attempts to combine their failed attempts to narrativize O'Malley's experience in the Caucasus with his own memories of conversations with O'Malley about this experience. He hopes that by means of these supplementary impressions the salvific content buried in the crazy pages of the notebooks can be rescued and made available to humanity at large, and so finally enable the reorientation of human sociality towards a larger form of shared life that was the project to which O'Malley had unsuccessfully devoted himself after his return from the Caucasus.

In 1800, Friedrich Kittler has argued, Nature is expressive, and the poet voices what it has to say; language is "only a channel, the true poet only a translator." In 1900, Nature is no longer transmitting; language consequently ceases to be a channel, and is downgraded to one medium among others. The figure of this de-sourcing of language is Nietzsche, the first, failed, philosopher of the typewriter, and the first "writer and nothing more." No longer a translator, a scribe, or an interpreter, Nietzsche in the clinic fills his notebooks with pages of writing exercises — mere writing, in its bare materiality as graphic inscription.

It is this condition that Blackwood, like other writers of the weird tale, grapples with in *The Centaur*. Almost every chapter has an epigraph that foregrounds the place of Nature in the discourse network of 1800. Novalis features in several of these, as does Gustav Fechner's effort to reconstitute the discourse network of 1800 as psychophysics in his *The Little Book of Life After Death*, although Schelling's *Naturphilosophie* would seem to be the ultimate point of reference for the panpsychism of *The Centaur* itself. In his abjection of O'Malley, Blackwood presents him as attuned to the wavelength of the earth, but requiring the intervention of his friend, the narrator, to transpose what he receives into the medium of writing. I do not mean, however, simply to subscribe Blackwood's novel at the critical juncture of discourse networks that Kittler has described, or even to demonstrate how gamely Blackwood grapples with this critical juncture in his redescription of Nature's voice as sound, pulse, current, and other such adumbrations of incipient contemporary technologies of communication. For I think *The Centaur* makes a more provocative intervention in our understanding of discourse networks and media theory.

The linkage of poet, Nature, and human past in *The Centaur* is operationalized by the presence of the relic. The relic is what should no longer be present in the present, as the leftover from some prior life world, but yet, as the uncanny persistence of what should no longer be here, continues to message us in its own, distinctive way. The relic is a modality of communication that operates as a supervenient channel, a ghost channel, whose presence is no longer explicable according to the logic of the discourse network.

The relic makes a disguised appearance in *Discourse Networks* in the figure of magic. Kittler notes that "magical or theological untranslatability was an ancient topos that became fashionable again circa 1900," and observes that in the contemporary discourse network magical spells or incantations appear as "isolated, foreign bodies," where they appear alongside entire artificial languages that were deliberately created. As Kittler's own example of the latter indicates, however — a faux-Rhenish hosanna from Stefan George's "Origins" that sounds "süss und befeurend wie Attikas choros" — these foreign bodies may not be strays from the future at all, but rather specially marked instances of the more general phenomenon of the relic, and all the more obviously so when they are invented for their occasion so as to provide the relic with the largest arena available for communicative interpellation.

How, then, does the relic interpellate us? Historical philology asserts that the remains of antiquity can only be properly encountered as what once had their place in a historical human life world, and that this life world as it is reconstructed by historical philology is the only channel on which we can properly view them. On other channels they appear staticky, blurred, or impoverished, and it is only when they are reintegrated into an imagined form of life that we see them as they really are. Historical philologists operationalize the communicative potential of the relics of historical life worlds.

In this respect, historical philology works like historical ecology, for which all forms of life are to be experienced as vestiges of the scene of their emergence. What we saw in Leopold and Roosevelt is that hauntological projections of such scenes allow human beings to spectate on their own lost primordial possibilities. The relic invites us to consider the kinds of experience that once existed alongside it, but are disenacted in the present, and so invites us to intimate reflections on the desirability of possible forms of life. The special appeal of the relic emerges from the relationship between intimacy and isolation in the way that it communicates with us. Because it supervenes upon the logic of the discourse network it is a figure of interpellation. It reconstitutes the discourse network as a modality of impoverishment with respect to itself.

So centaurs, in *The Centaur*, are outcomes of the world soul in its primal phase of creativity — "survivals of her early life," projections, emanations, and self-externalizations of the Earth's consciousness that are apprehensible by human beings in the present who themselves possess some element of these Urmenschen by which they are able to divine their presence. O'Malley is compared to a "faun" stranded in modernity. Relic resonates with relic, ghost calls out to ghost.

The call of the Urwelt reaches the relics of the Urmenschen via a "channel to the Earth's fair youth, a channel for some reason still unclosed." This channel is located near the Cycladic islands — by Tinos, in fact — and when O'Malley and his companions tune themselves to its frequency, what they receive is "a Message, a Summons, a Command that somehow held entreaty at its heart." Its syllables are "mothered" by the sea and air and its content is a single sound: "Chiron!" In its recoding of Nature's maternal voice as signal, channel, and noise, *The Centaur* enacts the communicative modalities of the weird tale that David Toop describes in *Sinister Resonance* under the rubric of the spectral: background vocalizations of nonhuman life that, most of the time, we successfully tune out, but to which, under certain conditions, we may become attuned, with unhappy consequence for our ordinary psychic functioning.

H. P. Lovecraft's "The Whisperer in the Darkness" is perhaps the best example of what the weird tale does with this possibility. Its opening sentence — "Bear in mind closely that I did not see any actual visual horror at the end" — is a teaser for horrors to come that are adumbrated by the reader especially as sounds. Nathaniel Hawthorne's "Roger Malvin's Burial" is a foundational precursor for the weird tale in this regard. A nonhuman voice guides the hapless Reuben Bourne into the forest to kill his own son, just as, in *The Centaur*, spiritual guidance by aural means is literalized in O'Malley's growing awareness as he nears his goal of "a distinct guidance, even of direction as to his route of travel."

In the weird tale, tuning to the frequency of the nonhuman means death, and this is also true in *The Centaur*, where, as the psychiatrist Stahl never tires of reminding O'Malley, becoming centaur is not only an escape from civilization's demon song of terror and desolation into the de-individuation of the primal herd, but also actually, literally, death. The older Russian passenger dies on board ship, and the split second, full body experience of becoming-centaur that O'Malley has when he meets him in centaur form, which unfolds in the time that it takes his Georgian guide to complete a single hand gesture, is a near-death experience from which he is able to extricate himself only just in the nick of time.

What Bernie Krause, in *The Great Animal Orchestra*, calls "geophony" — the deep sonic background of earth noise that is primordially prior to animal sounds — appears in *The Centaur* as the fulfillment of a recognizable trajectory of the weird tale, in which the voice of the nonhuman is the agent of a lethal antipathy to human life — the vengeful spirit of the forest that manifests itself as an inner voice in Hawthorne's "Roger Malvin's Burial," the alien life form in Lovecraft's "The Whisperer in the Darkness," and the pagan Nature divinity of Roman Britain in Arthur Machen's *The Hill of Dreams*.

On the other hand, *The Centaur* also reaches back behind the weird tale to what Toop has called the "preternatural hearing" of James Fenimore Cooper's wilderness novels, in which there is an effort to capture not only the look of the American wilderness, but also its sound. In *The Last of the Mohicans*, in particular, Cooper defers visualization to the reader in the thematization of tracking. The miraculous rescues accomplished by Hawkeye and the Indian scouts afford a vicarious experience of what it would be like to be able to find one's way in the wilderness through visual clues thanks to the enhanced visual acuity that comes from living in, and off, the forest. Sound, however, remains the prerogative of authorial ambition — the ambition to replicate the hearing of the novel's indigenous inhabitants, for whom to hear is to encounter the source of sound without the need for a secondary visualization on the basis of the sound. It is the expression of living with the forest, an attempt to body forth the "breathing silence" of the American wilderness as the distinctive soundscape of the novel. It is here, as much as in its characterology, that *The Last of the Mohicans* realizes its author's aspirational claim that "the business of a writer of fiction is to approach, as near as his powers will allow, to poetry."

The Centaur signals the Americanness of the Caucasus as a kind of ur-Greece in a chapter epigraph from Thoreau's *Walden*, and, more immediately, in a comparison of O'Malley's newfound guidance by Nature with the life of the American Indian:

In common with animal, bird, and insect life, all intimately close to Nature, he began to feel as realities those subtle currents of the Earth's personality by which the seals know direction in the depths of a thousand-mile sea, by which the homing pigeons blaze trails through space, birds fly south, the wild bees know their pathways, and all simple life, from the Red Indian to the Red Ant, acknowledges the viewless guidance of the mother's enveloping heart. The cosmic life ran through his being, lighting signals, offering service, more

— claiming leadership.

Indeed, O'Malley as faun may best be understood in reference to Hawthorne's *The Marble Faun*, whose title in England was *The Transformation*, and in whose title character Europe's deep classical past is figured with the traits of the American Indian, just as the indigenous Caucasians of *The Centaur* retain possession of what was common to the American Indian and the primordial Greek.

A channel open to techno-archaic messaging from the primordial source of life produces dancing, the movement of animals, and the wordless understanding of early humanity, and the novel gestures towards its own openness to this connection by signaling its desire to become something other than prose. O'Malley is sure that language cannot capture a form of life that flourished before language existed, but his narrator believes he can stage "essential inarticulateness struggling into an utterance foreign to it." One obstacle he must cope with in trying to realize this ambition is his understanding that O'Malley's reintegration into primordial life involved him in an experience of time that cannot be captured in the modes of human narrativity that are ready to hand. To accommodate the absence of "climax, in the story-book meaning," he must open his prose to the eternal in shared life, like a monk "for whose heart a hundred years had passed while he listened to the singing of a little bird." Whereas geophony is the voice of danger, biophony is what *The Centaur* gestures at in order to communicate the experience of a consciousness that has become more capacious in its destructuration. Birdsong communicates the eternal of deep time through simple iteration, and the narrator's attempt to enact this possibility in a new kind of prose entails the decomposition of narrative into pictures:

He remembered, for instance, one definite picture: a hot

autumn sun upon a field of stubble where the folded corn-sheaves stood; thistles waving by the hedges; a yellow field of mustard rising up the slope against the sky-line, and beyond a row of peering elms that rustled in the wind. The beauty of the little scene was somehow poignant. He recalled it vividly. It had flamed about him, transfiguring the world; he had trembled, yearning to see more, for just behind it he divined with an exulting passionate worship this gorgeous, splendid Earth-Being with whom at last he now actually moved. In that instant of a simple loveliness her consciousness had fringed his own — had bruised it. He had known it only by the partial channels of sight and smell and hearing, but had felt the greater thing beyond, without being able to explain it. And a portion of what he felt had burst in speech from his lips...The memory fled away. He shook himself free of it. Then others came in its place, another and another, not all with people, blind, deaf, and unreceptive, yet all of "common," simple scenes of beauty when something vast had surged upon him and broken through the barriers that stand between the heart and Nature. Such curious little scenes they were. In most of them he had evidently been alone. But one and all had touched his soul with a foretaste of this same nameless ecstasy that now he knew complete. In every one the Consciousness of the Earth had "bruised" his own.

The narrator renders O'Malley's disarticulated consciousness as an iteration of the occasions that anticipated the connectedness he would eventually experience in the Caucasus. Rather than attempting to become sound, like birdsong, in order to communicate the salvific destructuration of O'Malley's mind, the narration analogizes the experience of biophonic sound by becoming imagistic and poem-like. As the writing suggests the experience of psychic restructuring by gesturing at medial transformation, the justice of Lovecraft's observations on *The*

Centaur becomes apparent: "A close and palpitant *approach* to the inmost substance of dream...[that] works enormous havoc with the conventional barriers between reality and imagination."

The writing is an approach, not an arrival, and it is illuminating to compare the thematization of non-realization in *The Centaur* with its thematization in Arthur Machen's *The Hill of Dreams*. The protagonist of that book, Lucian Taylor, moves to London in the aftermath of his geophonic interpellation by a pagan Nature divinity, where we are led to believe that he is hard at work on a masterpiece of decadent writing that will give poetic realization to his drug-fueled nocturnal rambles through the growing city of London. At his death, however, his landlady discovers a volume of writing in his room that consists of nothing but meaningless scribbles. Like Nietzsche at his writing exercises, or the "all work and no play makes Jack a dull boy" scene at the typewriter in Stanley Kubrick's *The Shining*, this is a moment when writing is exposed as mere graphism. But in the type scene in *The Centaur*, when O'Malley's landlady discovers the sack of his notebooks, the dead writer has a postmortem interpreter at hand to take on the task of turning the barely comprehensible manuscripts that result from his geophonic interpellation into a readable text. As at Delphi, transposition is a second operation that turns what would otherwise be mere graphism into communication, thereby demonstrating the reality, and the truth, of the supervenient channel.

For his interpreter, our narrator, it is the very failure of O'Malley's "mad campaign" to convince the world of the need to change its form of life by producing a convincing account of what he experienced in the Caucasus that is the index of the genuineness of his "blinding and unutterable Dream." It is not the great poets, but "especially the little poets who cannot utter half the fire that consumes them," who know "the searing pain and passion and the true inwardness of it all." Blackwood turns the pathos of non-realization that makes the conclusion of

Machen's *The Hill of Dreams* so heartbreaking into an index of the Real. O'Malley's isolation is the strandedness of the centaurs themselves as subjects and expressions of a relictualized primordial life, but the really critical point for the novel's operationalization of this life is that its apprehension no longer requires that language be understood as unmediated translation of what is seen and heard on the centaur channel. Secondary realization allows for the operation of the supervenient channel as a visionary experience that language acknowledges in transmedial gestures but does not transmit, or translate:

> Standing aloof from all the rest, in isolation, *like dreams in a poet's mind, too potent for expression*, they thus knew tragedy — the tragedy of long neglect and loneliness. Seated on peak and ridge, rising beyond the summits in the clouds, filling the valleys, spread over watercourse and forest, they passed their life of lonely majesty — apart, *their splendor too remote for him as yet to share*. Long since had Earth withdrawn them from the hearts of men. Her lesser children knew them no more. But still through the deep recesses of her further consciousness they thundered and were glad...*though few might hear that thunder, share that awful joy...*

Nature produces the centaurs as subjects of primordial experience that instantiate its own experience of itself. This is what O'Malley is unable to do in his writing, but the gap between his experience and his writing involves the narrator in a second order effort to realize what was apprehensibly present in O'Malley's living voice but has not been made available in his notebooks. Hölderlin, in "Das Belebende," poetizes that "the idea of centaurs must be that of the spirit of a river, insofar as it makes a way and a limit, with force, on the originally pathless, outward growing earth," and the narrator hits upon the same idea in his description of O'Malley's voice:

The litter of disordered notebooks filled to the covers with fragments of such beauty that they almost seem to burn with a light of their own, lies at this moment before me on my desk. I still hear the rushing torrent of his language across the spotted table-cloth in that dark restaurant corner. But the incoherence seems only to increase with my best efforts to combine the two. "Go home and dream it," as he said at last when I ventured a question here and there toward the end of the recital.

What a river makes in its passage is a bank, a strand — a reminder of its passage and a remainder of what has passed — a relic, like the luminous debris of O'Malley's writing. But a river is also a gateway to its primordial origination, if one can force one's way back upstream, against the current. It is this question of how to inhabit the relationship between source and relic, origination and remainder, that *The Centaur* wants us to tarry with. Voice and writing, stream and bank, cannot become the objects of a single cognition, and it is the impossibility of inhabiting them both at once that makes O'Malley an obstacle: both stranded and flowing, like the centaurs themselves.

The nature of the obstacle is manifested in the word that names what O'Malley underwent in the Caucasus: *At-one-ment.* Atonement is Lévi-Strauss's name for the project of depressive anthropology, but here it is a destructured, unsayable word. O'Malley is not reabsorbed into the original, pre-expressive plentitude of primordial Nature, nor does he make good, or offer restitution for, its forgetting by human beings. By the end of the narrative, in fact, the language of plenitude begins to alternate with the language of intermittence in the description of O'Malley, as the signal of the primordial begins to give out in his person and in his writing: "A sense of interval there was at any rate, a 'transition-blank,' — whatever that may mean — he phrased it in the writing."

O'Malley has already alerted the narrator to the impossibility of capturing his experience of time in the structures of novelistic temporality, and the glossing of his incomprehensible "transition-blank," with the ordinary temporality of "interval" acknowledges the hard core of incommunicability in the original experience that cannot be modulated into literary prose. The 'transition-blank' is interference, intermittence, or blockage of the original signal, and a strong hint that the salvific remainder of the primordial that persists in isolated pockets of the modern world cannot be recovered as the basis of a new form of life actuated by the event of reception. Instead we lock eyes with Greece as the parting look of the primordial, the last form of Western sociality in which a trace of the human being as a form of Nature's self-externalization can yet be discerned:

> The land toward which the busy steamer moved he knew, of course, was but the shell from which the inner spirit of beauty once vivifying it had long since passed away. Yet it remained a clue. That ancient loveliness, as a mood of the earth's early consciousness, was buried, not destroyed. Eternally it still flamed somewhere. And, long before the days of Greece, he knew, it had existed in yet fuller and more complete manifestation: that earliest, vastly splendid Mood of the earth's soul, too mighty for any existence that the history of humanity can recall, and too remote for any but the most daringly imaginative minds even to conceive. The Urwelt Mood, as Stahl himself admitted, even while it called to him, was a reconstruction that to men today could only seem — dangerous.

The Centaur offers a number of variations on the theme of being with primordial Nature: feeling with, seeing with, growing with, sharing with. But it is in its staging of a person struggling to enact his feelings for a plenitude that has been evacuated from the life world of the present that the novel really excels. O'Malley suffers with Nature through its own diminishment as the mature Thoreau would suffer with the woods of *Walden* after histories of early New England had revealed to him their pre-Columbian fullness: "Is it not a maimed and imperfect nature that I am conversant with?"

But if Blackwood has one eye on America in *The Centaur* all along, why is Greek mythology the vehicle for imagining the fading of its primordial life? The best answer, unsurprisingly, is the one that the book itself provides. As O'Malley sets off for the mountains of the Caucasus in search of the Urwelt whose traces in the Greek imagination are the source of its continuing attraction for Western modernity, he takes Jason as his precursor in this quest:

> Here, where the Argonauts once landed, the Golden Fleece still shone o' nights in the depths of the rustling beech woods; along the shores of that old Phasis their figures might still be seen, tall Jason in the lead, erect and silvery, passing o'er the shining, flowered fields upon their quest of ancient beauty. Further north from this sunny Colchian strand rose the peak of Kasbek, gaunt and desolate pyramid of iron, "sloping through five great zones of climate," whence the ghost of Prometheus still gazed down from his "vast frozen precipice" upon a world his courage would redeem. For somewhere here was the cradle of the human race, fair garden of some Edened life before the "Fall," when the Earth sang for joy in her first, golden youth, and her soul expressed itself in mighty forms that remain for lesser days but a faded hierarchy of visioned gods.

In a sublime act of literary haunting, *The Centaur* is possessed by the Greeks' own sense of the loss of the primordial. The "quest of ancient beauty" that Jason leads is not so much the archaic myth of the Golden Fleece itself as it is its retelling in the *Argonautica*, a symptomatic manifestation of the Hellenistic Greeks' consciousness of the loss of naturalness in human life that Schiller points to in "On Naïve and Sentimental Poetry" as the originary moment that embarks Western sentimental consciousness on its quest for the recovery of Nature.

O'Malley's experience is one of radical alterity to language — "transition-blank" is a language erratic that experience leaves behind it as it pushes on, a word boulder around which the gloss of narration flows. By contrast, O'Malley's becoming-Jason — which is also Blackwood's becoming-Jason — supervenes upon this putative narrative structuration as the unaccountable experience of haunting. To be aware of the loss of plentitude, and to go in search of lost primordiality, is to be subject to haunting by prior experiences of loss in ways that are unaccountable — unnarratable — in the structures of psychic modulation that are ready to hand. *The Centaur* remains true to its allegiances with German *Naturphilosophie*. Nature is the ground of historical consciousness, and the loss of Greece as a historical form of human life figures the loss of the primordial whose parting glance can still be discerned in the remainders of this form of life. Yet *The Centaur* also remains true to its allegiances with the weird tale. Like the Nature of the weird tale, Greece is an agent in Blackwood's story — her ghosts occupy those who look to her for guidance, and she sets them on paths of her own choosing.

The hauntology of *The Centaur* is not just imaginative and characterological, but writerly: the narrative is a reconstitution of O'Malley's incomprehensible journal entries and inspirational conversation by a narrator who has, without any reasons being given, assumed the task of transmitting O'Malley's message to the world after O'Malley's death. As O'Malley, in setting himself to receive transmissions from the primordial, is subsumed into Jason as a condition of becoming-centaur, so the nameless narrator is possessed by O'Malley, and this possession is figured in Blackwood's haunted prose as the unacknowledged citations that are the connective tissue of the *Argonautica* passage, and its haunting by the late Romantic poetry it has for some reason survived.

Hauntology leaves its mark in *The Centaur* at each level of inscription. It is thematized in the becoming-centaur of O'Malley — his possession by the inoperable discourse of translation, which is then deferred to the editorial work of the narrator. And it appears as a cipher in its drifting, unassigned citations. The past imposes itself as an interpellation, an implicit instruction to suture these relics together so that they might be a permanent gateway to the past, rather than a fleeting portal wandering through the text. This is the spectral form of life of the relic, the relic that is where we find it, "sitting in a library, standing in a gallery, *wading through a crane marsh*, moving through a ruin." *The Centaur* is mythology reimagined by Ghost Box, "by turns joyous and at other times shot through with terror or supernatural wonder. Parallel world TV soundtracks and nostalgia for an imaginary past." Crucially, though, the relationship to this mythology is lived as shame. *The Centaur* is a hontology of human capabilities in the present as these are enacted along the axis of connectivity to living beings as a whole.

The Centaur signals the Americanness of the Caucasus as a kind of ur-Greece in a chapter epigraph from Thoreau's *Walden*, and by comparing the life of the Greeks to life with Mother Nature in America. But there is this difference. Whereas there are postindian warriors who battle the simulations of Indian hyperreality with trickster survivance, it is less obvious who the postgreek warriors are who battle the simulations of Hellenism. In the weird tale, the only alternative to the simulation is death, pure and simple. When O'Malley and his companions arrive in the Caucasus, they find a copy of Böcklin's "Centaur" already installed in a shop window. The locals point to the inscription beneath it, which they cannot read. But, we are told, for these mountain men of the Caucasus, "to see them [centaurs] is to die."

A bad trip is one that keeps coming back to itself. There is no painting by Böcklin called "Centaur." What they see is a simulation of the simulation. There is just the simulation, or death, either of which they could have had without leaving home. This is the story of Lucian Taylor, the writer hero of Arthur Machen's *The Hill of Dreams*. He meets a faun in a Roman hill fort in Wales and is overcome by him. He lives the life the faun gives him to lead in the person of Avallaunius, an imaginary inhabitant of the Roman town. He becomes "the realization of the vision of Caermaen," the scribal hand by which the faun tries to bring his simulation to life. Lucian's intimate spiritual guide in this project is Hawthorne. He seeks "the magic...by which Hawthorne had lit his infernal Sabbath fires, and fashioned a burning aureole about the village tragedy of *The Scarlet Letter*." When he is at a loss how to proceed, he transcribes one of Hawthorne's pages in an attempt to infuse his own writing with its power.

Lucian attempts to enact the historical form of life of the Roman city in his writing as a way of silencing the voice of the faun, which he identifies retrospectively as a geophonic interpellation — the "wood whisper" of the labyrinthine "mesh of the hills" from which he is trying to extricate himself. In so doing, he lives out in his own person the response to geophonic interpellation on the part of two of Hawthorne's characters — Reuben Bourne, who succumbs to the voice of the forest in "Roger Malvin's Burial," and his wife Dorcas, who drowns out her apprehension of its enchantment by singing it away:

Dorcas, after the departure of the two hunters, continued her preparations for their evening repast. Her sylvan table was the moss-covered trunk of a large fallen tree, on the broadest part of which she had spread a snow-white cloth and arranged what were left of the bright pewter vessels that had been her pride in the settlements. It had a strange aspect that one little spot of homely comfort in the desolate heart of Nature. The sunshine yet lingered upon the higher branches of the trees that grew on rising ground; but the shadows of evening had deepened into the hollow where the encampment was made, and the firelight began to redden as it gleamed up the tall trunks of the pines or hovered on the dense and obscure mass of foliage that circled round the spot. The heart of Dorcas was not sad; for she felt that it was better to journey in the wilderness with two whom she loved than to be a lonely woman in a crowd that cared not for her. As she busied herself in arranging seats of mouldering wood, covered with leaves, for Reuben and her son, her voice danced through the gloomy forest in the measure of a song that she had learned in youth. The rude melody, the production of a bard who won no name, was descriptive of a winter evening in a frontier cottage, when, secured from savage inroad by the high-piled snow-drifts, the family rejoiced by their own fireside. The whole song possessed the nameless charm peculiar to unborrowed thought, but four continually recurring lines shone out from the rest like the blaze of the hearth whose joys they celebrated. Into them, working magic with a few simple words, the poet had instilled the very essence of domestic love and household happiness, and they were poetry and picture joined in one. As Dorcas sang, the walls of her forsaken home seemed to encircle her; she no longer saw the gloomy pines, nor heard the wind which still, as she began each verse, sent a heavy breath through the branches, and died away in a hollow moan from the burden of the song.

The scene is a perfect miniature of human sociality as seclusion from shared life with living beings as a whole. The walls of humanness arise magically around Dorcas by the power of song, and she sings the forest away from her. She is unable to save her child, but she saves herself and Reuben. So, too, in Algernon Blackwood's "The Man Whom the Trees Loved," David Bittacy's wife is able to save her husband from the interpellation of the trees that surround their New Forest cottage by reestablishing the solidity of its walls as a defensive fortification against the "huge collective life" of the forest trees that try to win him "across the border — into themselves."

David Bittacy is made aware of his disposition to interpellation by the forest by the work of a painter who has an uncanny power to relay shared life with trees as second person relationality, and who explains to David that the trees love him because of his natural disposition towards this form of life with them. "The authority of a host of trees" is, for David, "something not to be denied," whereas what saves Mrs. Bittacy, and prevents her from hearing "the wireless message from a vast Emitter" that the forest trees transmit to her husband, is that humanness appears in her as a kind of insulation from such messaging, an incapacity for attunement. The message does not reach her with full clarity because she is so deeply embedded in the counter-sociality of her shared life with human beings that the appeal of shared life with living beings as a whole is transformed in her into an anti-chorus. The "instinctive aversion she felt to being shut in" is the reflex of her own domesticity abjected on to nonhuman life.

It is this form of protection that Lucian Taylor is unable to enact for himself because when he thinks he is protecting himself from the call of nonhuman life he is actually reproducing it. Writing relays the voice of the faun whose vector Lucian has never ceased to be. It is the perduring form of his original interpellation. London, where Lucian flees to escape him, becomes a gigantic stage set in which he is doomed to perpetually reenact his experience at the fort as a drama of interpellation by beings to whom he is unable to respond with an answering "you." The city takes on the appearance of a labyrinth that is a vastly distended amplification of the circular enclosure of the fort, and Lucian's deathbed vision of the failure of his life's work is the consummation of the inoperable apprehension of shared life that was gifted to him by the faun:

> Ring within ring the awful temple closed around him; unending circles of vast stones, circle within circle, and every circle less throughout all ages. In the center was the sanctuary of the infernal rite, and he was borne thither as in the eddies of a whirlpool, to consummate his ruin, to celebrate the wedding of the Sabbath. He flung up his arms and beat the air, resisting with all his strength, with muscles that could throw down mountains; and this time his little finger stirred for an instant, and his foot twitched upon the floor.

Lucian's bodily gestures are a precise analogical measure of the gap between ambition and realization in his journals, the neat pile of manuscript pages that are revealed by his landlady to be no more than "illegible hopeless scribblings" that nobody could read, even if they wanted to. The verdict is death by misadventure, but whereas the coroner sees opium as the lethal factor, we know that the real killer is the shame of life and Lucian's inability to produce an alternative — to expand and reattune his feeling for life along the axis of connectivity to living beings as a whole. Lucian submits to the hyperreal simulation of antiquity as an alternative to the scrutiny of others that he experiences as a condition of permanent ontic shame in the excruciating provincial sociality of a Welsh country town, and for that he dies. His story, too, is a hontology.

According to Heidegger, the *anthropos* — *Dasein* — is the being for whom its own being is and should be a care. According to the Crow, and to the Greeks too, the horse is the being for whom the being of others is a care. In the *Iliad*, it is only horses that register atrocity in general. Human beings react to this death and that death in which their own being is intimately involved, but horses register the scale of the event as a relation to atrocity in general, a settling in and sedimentation of the atrocity as a whole.

The *anthropos* and the horse come together in the centaur, where the figures of care are as uneasily conjoined as their two anatomies. The centaurs' violence is a poem, the original poem of force. They are "the wild beasts of the mountains" who fought with the strongest of men in ancient days. But Chiron is the epitome of gentleness. The huge centaur snuggles the young Achilles and the hero wraps his arms around him. Even when his mother is present he prefers the breast he knows.

Achilles remembers the centaur on his way to Troy, to the deaths of men and horses: "Father taught me how to travel through the wilderness with him. He had big steps. I didn't cry when rocks smashed to pieces in the creeks. The silence of the forest didn't scare me. When I was twelve I could outrun deer and horses. Chiron used to chase me through canyons and when we were done he would carry me on his shoulders. I can't quite remember what it was like. Once he made me stand in the river in winter. He didn't used to kiss me unless I came home covered in blood. My mother knows the rest." They can't quite remember what it was like, their poem. "What other baby grew up crawling through freshly dug snow?" Chiron wonders.

Friedrich Hölderlin remembers the centaurs as the onset of enlivening force:

The concept of centaurs is probably the spirit of a stream, as long as the railway makes a border, by force, on the originally pathless, monitored earth. His image is therefore at points of Nature, where the shore is rich as to rocks and grottoes, particularly in places where originally leaving the current chain of mountains it had to tear through their direction transverse, and in caves of the earth for lactating animals. The waters were craving their direction, broke through at a point where the mountains that included him most easily hung together. The designed wave pushed the rest of the pond, and the way of life on the banks changed to the assault of the forest. True centaur songs are sung with the spirit of the river, as the Greek Chiron also taught Achilles the strings.

The Crow remember their horses as beings for whom the being of others is a care:

> To the Crow a horse is everything. It's in your blood. When I was growing up a horse was always there that you could ride and you'd play with the horse all your life to where you can trust a horse, to where your shadow and the horse's shadow are one.
>
> I have been told that the white man, who is almost a god, and yet a great fool, does not believe that the horse has a spirit [soul]. This cannot be true. I have many times seen my horse's soul in his eyes. And this day on that knoll I knew my horse understood. I saw his soul in his eyes.

N. Scott Momaday, who calls the form of life of the Plains Indians horse nations "centaur culture," tells of a hunting horse that died of shame. He also tells of Buffalo Bill and Secretariat, and the exotic old people of his tribe, who spoke only Kiowa, wore their hair in braids, and imaged for him the "bygone and infinitely exciting time of the centaurs." Which is also the time of care:

> Edward Curtis preserved for us the unmistakable evidence of our involvement in the universe. Curtis was acutely alive to evanescence; indeed, in a real sense it is his subject. The portraits here are of people whose way of life is coming rapidly to an end. We see the full awareness of this in their

eyes. And yet these visages are not to be defined in terms of despair. Rather, there is a general information of fortitude, patience, and something like assent, and above all composure and valor. In the face of such a man as Slow Bull, for example, there seem etched the very principles of the warrior ideal: bravery, steadfastness, generosity, and virtue. We do not doubt that he is real in his mind and heart, in his word and in his vision. The same can be said of the portraits of Red Cloud, Chief Joseph, and Bear's Belly — in his bear robe — there is an amalgam of man and wilderness, an equation that is a definition of the American Indian in relation to nature. And yet, in all of these photographs there is a privacy so profound as to be inviolable. A Navajo weaver sits at her loom before a canyon wall. She is a silhouette; her loom is a geometry that seems essential to her being, organic, the extension of her hands into the earth itself. A young girl in her finery stands before her play tipi; she is every young girl who has ever lived upon the earth.

An amalgam: a centaur in the flesh. Henry David Thoreau imagined that "the rays of Greek poetry struggle down to us, and mingle with the sunbeams of the recent day." And here in fact they do. Poetry is storage, preservation, transmission. What it saves warms us, but as tranquility — so serenely that we hardly detect its enlivening power: "It is not the overflowing of life but its subsidence rather, and is drawn from under the feet of the poet. It is enough if Homer but say the sun sets."

3

Autarky and incoherent care

Optimism is erotic and totalizing. Pessimism is anerotic and fragmentary. As Joshua Dienstag shows in *Pessimism*, the discourse of pessimism tends to incoherence as a result of its own lack of faith in solutions, totalizing or otherwise. Its most characteristic form is the aphorism, which can hardly stand up to the relentless outpouring of positive solutions from a society committed to working out its own future as a project capable of realization. As Eric Voegelin argued in *Science, Politics & Gnosticism*, our supposedly secular modernity remains entirely eschatological in this respect, committed to the image of a world prison from which it is obligatory for human beings to try to free themselves simply because they are human beings, and unlike anything else in the cosmos.

In *The Centaur* and *The Hill of Dreams*, zeroing in on a text in ruins gestures at the possibility of a new kind of writing. Its latency is not that of a fragment that points to a whole unrealizable under present circumstances. The aspirations of the maker are suppressed or surpassed. A better analogy would be Martin Hannett's deathly makeover of the liveness of Joy Division's live sound: "There was a lot of space in [Joy Division's] sound. They were a gift to a producer, because they didn't have a clue. They didn't argue. *A Factory Sample* was the first thing I did with them. I think I'd had the new AMS delay line for about two weeks. It was called 'Digital'. It was heaven sent." The work in ruins, which does not even seem to bear within itself the possibility of a work, is something other than the fragment that could have been part of a whole but isn't. Like the aphorism that is only efficacious in the moment of its pessimistic uptake, the latency of the work in ruins invites its realization in the hands of others.

Lyric poetry is often like this. The obvious analogy with song is that it doesn't make much sense until you make it your own:

Then it often seems to him the best,
Almost completely forgotten there,
Where the beam does not burn,
In the shadow of the woods
By Lake Bienne to be in fresh green,
And carefree poor in tones,
Like beginners to learn from nightingales

This is Hölderlin, in "The Rhine," on Rousseau's island life. Despite its modest appearance, to learn from nightingales as if we were beginners is an exorbitant demand. It requires a strongly willed return to an imagined beginning, to the possibility of beginning again, that, as Gianni Vattimo argues, is a dream that Western thought has had the greatest difficulty in allowing to fade in the light of the waking realization that "there are no transcendental conditions of possibility for experience which might be attainable through some type of reduction or *epoché*, suspending our ties to historical-cultural, linguistic, and categorical horizons."

Vattimo would put a nail in the coffin of the depressive anthropology that has fueled the dream of starting over from Rousseau to Hölderlin and Lévi-Strauss. What he would put in its place is a new form of care. The winding down of the dream that is what Vattimo calls "weak thought" has as one of its tasks the recognition that the mining of antiquity for the handful of thin concepts that have been extracted from it without any real regard for the site of their origination — freedom, democracy, reason, science, beauty — leaves in its wake a slag heap of useless spoil for historians and philologists to pore over in their efforts to reconstruct the "lived experience of the past" — the context of culture from which these concepts have been dug out.

But the idea that these concepts can be reinstalled in their original form of historical life as living ideas is every bit as factitious as their extraction. What remains of the past is simply remains. Both the remainder and the history of how it came to be remaindered engender a mild curiosity about what has come down to us as notionally our own, the history to which we understand ourselves to belong. This is what Vattimo calls *Andenken*, after what Hölderlin, in a less ambitious moment, names as a turning towards what is left, without the hope that what is gone is within our power to recall:

> *But now those men*
> *are gone to Indians,*
> *there at the airy headland*
> *of the vine hills, where*
> *the Dordogne descends*
> *and together with the glorious*
> *Garonne the stream flows out*
> *ocean-wide. The sea takes away*
> *memory and also gives it back,*
> *and love too lifts up the eyes assiduously,*
> *but what remains, poets tend to that.*

Poets cannot bring back the past, they can only care for what remains. Imagine a box of old letters or childhood photos. You carry it around with you from apartment to apartment, house to house, because you can't quite bring yourself to get rid of it. You don't have an active relationship with it, even as memories, but you are still attached to it. What was once fully animated, a repository of the living concerns that make up a life as it is unfolding, has slowly faded over the years. The life has gone out of it, so that all that remains is the fact of attachment itself. It no longer even stands for the passage of time. At the moment the last life left it, it ceased to be a marker of time, and persists instead by merely being there.

Andenken is a way of being with the things of the past that is an acceptance of their dormancy in contrast to what they were and might have been for us, and of our own limitation in respect to the roads not traveled that they represent. Its curation has an active dimension, although it is drastically limited in comparison to *poiesis*, and is also somewhat random and incoherent in its mode of operation. Consider Lars von Trier's *Melancholia* as a film about what to do in the face of the end of the world.

A planet by the name of Melancholia enters earth's solar system from behind the sun. It draws ever closer to the earth, but then appears to be passing it by, only to return and crash into it. The film looks at how different people respond to the impending catastrophe and, in particular, the contrasting responses of two sisters — Justine, whose failed wedding occupies the first half of the film, and Claire, who hosts the wedding in her country house, which is where the two sisters subsequently await Melancholia's arrival. Justine's co-workers play their part in the wedding drama, but the second half is just Justine, Claire, and her family — her husband, her young son, and their horses, who await the end of the world with varying degrees of open-mindedness and clear-sightedness.

The husband is disposed of early in the proceedings. Once he realizes that the scientists have got it wrong, and Melancholia won't be the aesthetically pleasing and scientifically informative fly-by he had been promised, he kills himself with the anti-depressants that Claire had put aside to alleviate her own anxiety. Claire's approach is to try to do the right thing. She covers up her husband's body so no one will discover it, and makes it look as if he has ridden off in search of help. She then tries to escape with her son, and when this plan fails she suggests to Justine that they await the advent of Melancholia with a glass of wine on the garden terrace.

Justine thinks this is a terrible idea. Justine is persistently depressed. She has already terminated her marriage and her career, so it is not a huge surprise when she tells Claire that life on earth is evil and no one will miss it. The film's surprise ending, then, is that in the moments before Melancholia's arrival, it is Justine who takes charge of the end of life for herself, for Claire, and for Claire's son. She who had seemed to be beyond care becomes an accomplished caregiver. She had promised Claire's son they would build a magic cave in the course of her visit, and she now makes good on this promise. They gather sticks from the woods together, which the child sharpens with a pocketknife, and they then fit these sticks together to make a tipi frame. The film ends with Justine, Claire, and her son sitting inside the uncovered tipi frame as Melancholia enters the earth's atmosphere, consuming everything in its path.

From a practical perspective, Claire's wanting to do the right thing represents the pointlessness of mourning when there is no possibility of a future in which the outcome of mourning could be enacted as an alternative to the endlessness of melancholy. But why does Justine, the clear-sighted melancholic, build a tipi? Its uselessness as a shelter is marked by the fact that, unlike a real tipi, it is not even covered. We watch Justine, Claire, and her son sitting inside it as Melancholia approaches. They close their eyes, but this is more a gesture of solidarity than self-defense, or even defensiveness. They see Melancholia, and it sees them, for the planet is invested with a brooding animacy by the *Liebestod* from Wagner's *Tristan and Isolde* that accompanies its every move.

Justine's tipi of twigs is a kind of ark. Her project is to transfer the work of interiority — the work of mourning — to the work of the hands. Justine and Claire's son build the tipi as a handicraft, a hunter-gatherer project, in contrast to the technoscience of Claire's husband, whose emblem is the telescope. His technoscience offers no affordances for continuing to live in a doomed world once its lack of practical utility is exposed. Justine manualizes the project of accommodation to the world without hoping that she is anything other than doomed. She moves conceptual making good into the work of the hands, and it is this insistence on building, making, and doing in all its manifest uselessness that makes what she does ark-building — the work of living on without the expectation that the world can be saved or made good.

Melancholia torques the affect of the sci-fi "when worlds collide" sub-genre towards a kind of comedy — cosmicomedy, we might call it — in Justine's refusal to mourn the imminent spectacle of the world's destruction by fire. The phenomenon to which the end of the film gives witness is what the Stoics called *ekpyrosis*: the world's inevitable consummation and self-fulfillment in the form of a fireball, to which philosophy's response is the genre of the *consolatio*, Stoicism's signature form. It is a consolation that changes nothing and helps very little. Just the opposite of a maximal solution, it offers becoming at peace with the inevitable as the little that philosophy has to offer — an ark of words, like Justine's ark of twigs. If mourning enacts a kind of radical hope, hope down to the wire, or hope against hope, in its elegiac effusions about life about to be lost, the Stoic's ataraxia is grounded in the refusal of this hope, accepting the inevitability of catastrophe as what has to be faced.

Melancholia points to the space of incoherent care that pessimism opens up. The past is never dead. It's not even past. Just when you think the malevolent planet is a lump of space rock passing in the night, back it comes to destroy you, apparently with a will of its own. Justine's response is depressive realism, to be sure, but, like survivance, it is a form of depressive realism that actually helps with living. It can cope with the presence of the past, because it understands the impossibility of ever really beginning over. Justine is a kind of Prospero, whose care for others is grounded in the melancholy understanding that you bring your past with you wherever you go, like it or not, as something you have to live with. Justine's incoherent gestures of care contrast with the fragments of Claire's moral simulation that point towards a philosophy of life she is unable to enact.

Incoherent care as a way of coping with the impact of the past is a signature gesture among the artists of Arte Povera. In the face of post-war American art's turn away from the past, Arte Povera engaged profoundly with the ideas of Nature, Mythology, and Life that shaped depressive anthropology's desire to begin again. But it did so calmly, as a fact of inheritance and survivance. It was neither spellbound nor traumatized by its engagement with what already occupied the field of culture.

Take, for instance, Michelangelo Pistoletto's "Venus of rags" — a mica-covered cement reproduction of a classical Venus, face-to-face with a colorful heap of rags. Naïve juxtaposition makes a way of experiencing inheritance as remainders, remnants that do not gesture at a putative whole. Instead of thrownness, we have thrownawayness — not an imperative to make sense of our situation, but an invitation to exercise our feelings of care for what precedes us in the world, what preoccupies the space of life before our own arrival on the scene.

The theatricality of "Venus of rags" stages the possibility of a mind going outside itself in the encounter with two kinds of relictualized objects — the remnants of the past in the form of a poor quality reproduction of an ancient art work, and the relics of the present in the form of the refuse of industrial production. The Venus reunites the rags and puts them in order. It triggers a "formal illumination" that is an opening for care, the creation of a threshold in which care can emerge. The space of their being together, and of our being there together with them, is a threshold of survivance, two mutually illuminating instances of belonging together that inter-animate one another. What would otherwise be an ugly reproduction and a discarded pile of old clothes together bring care to life as the supervenience of an unanticipated awareness of shared life.

The "Venus of rags" is an iconic realization of Arte Povera's attraction to energy, animation, and life through formal reduction, material austerity, and impoverished ideation. It works because it interpellates the viewer to occupy the space of inter-animacy in which the statue and the clothing give life to one another. The staging of being together as shared life animates and illuminates what would otherwise be unilluminated, disenlivened, and forgotten — on the one hand, ancient ideas of beauty, as they linger on in one place or another, on the other, the rags of society.

The exorbitant demand of mythology rests on the further exorbitant demand that everything in life is alive — that we inhabit a living cosmos, if only we could see it and feel it as such. Giuseppe Penone faces this demand calmly, as the call for literal repetition of the processes by which the living cosmos has come into being. In "Tree," he excavates the incipient branches of a living tree from a plank of industrial lumber. Or he makes a stone from stone, because literal repetition is what living Nature demands:

The stone that was alive and took part in the great life of the mountain, in the variation of its material and its structure, when broken away becomes a dead element suspended in time while awaiting its own perfection. The life of the river is able to quicken the time of the stone, carrying it more rapidly toward its state of rest. It is not possible to think of or to work the stone in a way that is different from that of the river. The blow of the point, chisel, peg, or bit, whetstones and sandpaper are all the tools of the river. Picking up a stone sculpted by the river, following the river upstream and discovering the point on the mountain where the stone came from, taking a new block of stone from the mountain, and making from it an exact replica of the stone taken from the river, means being a river. To produce a stone made of stone is perfect sculpture, it is a return to nature, a cosmic fortune, pure creation. The natural quality of good sculpture takes it on at cosmic value. It is being a river that is the true stone sculpture.

Penone accepts the exorbitant idea of life as something he can work with and work out, in extraordinarily demonstrative, exorbitantly demanding, gestures of care. Tradition is the name we have for our awareness of the slow disanimation of what is stored under the name of value, the leakage of life from what was once the site of a genial engagement. But disanimation is not the end of care, and the incoherence of our care for the things we care for need not necessarily be depressive either.

It is no accident that Arte Povera originated in Italy, in the ancient cities of Rome, Turin, Genoa, and Milan, where the presence of the past is unlikely to be overvalued, or even particularly coveted, for its potential to reanimate the present. The ubiquity of antiquity in such places de-singularizes the art object at the moment of its appearance so that it already appears in this moment as the topmost layer in an accretion or stratification of productive energy. It is illuminated by the light of its own passage into the past, the force of its energetic emergence already leaking out of it into the bed of remains into which it will soon subside and among which it will soon subsist, as another layer to be grown over and ground under.

Andenken is curatorial care, care for what was here before us, as a weak form of shared life with the past. It is weak but joyful, enthusiastic in its involvement with the past. Since it no longer has the responsibility for reanimating the present, it no longer has the obligation to make sense of the past. It is free to be quizzical and curious, not foundational, in its relationality — touching and letting go according to the transience of care. It has shed hermeneutic responsibility as a task imposed, in favor of a return to life, as this life is enacted in momentary experiences of tangency that cannot be sustained. Like Justine's ark, it transfers the work of interiority to the work of the hands.

In this respect, Andenken is a project of autarky, just as much as Rousseau's island, or Theodore Kaczynski's cabin. Autarky is only a question about social relations insofar as it is at first a question about capability loss and the outsourcing of the power to decide our own needs. Andenken means an end to the instrumentalization of the past, and the beginning of care for what we care for simply because we have taken it upon ourselves to care for it. Recovering the abrogated pleasure in the sentiment of our own existence begins with understanding our own needs, and the first step in understanding our own needs is finding out what we care for. It is to this desire that Rousseau attributes the origins of depressive anthropology, and it is for this reason that Andenken as a mode of care is its natural successor:

> When I have set out to learn something, my aim has been to gain knowledge for myself and not to be a teacher; I have always thought that before instructing others one should begin by knowing enough for one's own needs, and of all the studies I have undertaken in my life among men, there is hardly one that I would not equally have undertaken if I had been confined to a desert island for the rest of my days.

Notes and references

1. The shame of life

More than a year ago: Jacques Derrida, *Specters of Marx: The State of the Debt, the Work of Mourning and the New International* (New York: Routledge, 1993), 2. *He would have diagnosed today*: 49. *Someone, you or me, comes forward*: xvi. The corresponding passages in the original French edition are Jacques Derrida, *Spectres de Marx: L'État de la dette, le travail du deuil et la nouvelle Internationale* (Paris: Galilée, 1993), 22, 73, 13.

There will never be another New World: Claude Lévi-Strauss, *Tristes tropiques* (London: Penguin, 1992), 393. On Rousseau and the anthropological project: 389–92, 414. On the Nambikwara: 316–7.

Duties and natural needs: Jean-Jacques Rousseau, *The Discourses and Other Early Political Writings* (Cambridge: Cambridge University Press, 1997), 16. *Ataraxia*: 186–7. *There is, I sense, an age*: 133. *It is by dint of studying man*: 124. *The men we have before our eyes*: 138. On his sources: 209–10. *Carrying all of himself along with him*: 135.

Inventions of tribal cultures: Gerald Vizenor, *Manifest Manners: Narratives on Postindian Survivance* (Lincoln, NE: University of Nebraska Press, 1994), 13. *Native American Indian imagination*: 76.

This was how it would have seemed: D'Arcy McNickle, *The Surrounded* (Albuquerque: University of New Mexico Press, 2003), 116. *For the first time*: 74. *He too belonged*: 275. *How much greater*: 286. *Were not real people*: 62. *In the end he wore her down*: 240–2. "Violent-care" is a term coined by Thom Van Dooren in *Flight Ways: Life and Loss at the Edge of Extinction* (New York: Columbia University Press, 2014) to describe how captive animals from endangered species are made to survive, whether they like it or not.

A cow horse: James Welch, *Winter in the Blood* (New York:

Penguin, 1974), 114–15. *Oyáte*, "people," or "nation," is a regular term for other animals among the Lakota. As Tim Ingold observes in *Perception of the Environment: Essays in Livelihood, Dwelling and Skill* (London: Routledge, 2000), 49, such terminology among hunting cultures is unlikely to be a projection of their own social ambience onto "the mirror of nature," which is then somehow forgotten or disavowed as a projection, but is rather an acknowledgment of the ways in which other animals live in social groups like those of human beings.

Linderman also stands out: As Colin Calloway observes in *Our Hearts Fell to the Ground: Plains Indian Views of How the West Was Lost* (Boston: Bedford/St. Martin's Press, 1996), 25–6.

Suddenly, as though some medicine: Frank Linderman, *Pretty-shield: Medicine Woman of the Crows* (Lincoln, NE: University of Nebraska Press, 2003), 62–3. Her rejection of Linderman's interpretation is a rejection of what Tim Ingold, in *Perception of the Environment*, 24–5, calls sentient ecology: the "skills, sensitivities and orientations that have developed through long experience of conducting one's life in a particular environment," and that may be communicated to others as the speech of animals, without ascribing to them an intention to communicate. On Pretty-shield's relationship with Linderman, see Alma Hogan Snell, *Grandmother's Grandchild: My Crow Indian Life* (Lincoln, NE: University of Nebraska Press, 2000), 15–17, 71–2. Pretty-shield's attitude to writing is similar to that of Luther Standing Bear in *Land of the Spotted Eagle* (Lincoln, NE: University of Nebraska Press, 2006), 249: a desire that future generations of Lakota children should have the chance to grow up Lakota motivates his own decision to commit his self-experience to writing.

Man's first sentiment: Jean-Jacques Rousseau, *The Discourses and Other Early Political Writings* (Cambridge: Cambridge University Press, 1997), 161. *How are we to imagine*: 219. *Night was coming on*: Jean-Jacques Rousseau, *Reveries of the Solitary Walker* (Harmondsworth: Penguin, 1979), 39. *The feeling of existence*: 89.

The other members of the fauna: Aldo Leopold, *A Sand County Almanac* (Oxford: Oxford University Press, 1949), 96–7. *I do not understand*: Theodore Roosevelt, *Letters. Volume 2: 1898–1900* (Cambridge, MA: Harvard University Press, 1951), 948. *The absence of mammoths*: Paul Martin, *Twilight of the Mammoths: Ice Age Extinctions and the Rewilding of America* (Berkeley: University of California Press, 2007), 55. On genetically engineered centaurs, see Lee Silver, *Challenging Nature: The Clash Between Biotechnology and Spirituality* (New York: HarperCollins, 2007), 309–4. For Eduardo Kac's "Natural History of the Enigma," see http://www.ekac.org/nat.hist.enig.html

In my life in the woods: Theodore Kaczynski, *Technological Slavery* (Port Townsend, WA: Feral House, 2010), 405–6. On green anarchism, colonial era white flight, and taking back the *serious, practical, purposeful, life-and-death aspects* of life, see 130, 289–90, 385.

2. Greeks, Indians, and the weird tale

He was all man: Cited by Gerald Vizenor, *Manifest Manners: Narratives on Postindian Survivance* (Lincoln, NE: University of Nebraska Press, 1994), 32. *I shall suppose myself*: Jean-Jacques Rousseau, *The Discourses and Other Early Political Writings* (Cambridge: Cambridge University Press, 1997), 133. *Sparta*: 14.

Too subtle, perhaps: H. P. Lovecraft, *At the Mountains of Madness* (New York: Random House, 2005), 166.

Only a channel: Friedrich Kittler, *Discourse Networks 1800/1900* (Stanford: Stanford University Press, 1990), 73. On Nietzsche and the typewriter, 181–2. On Fechner, Nature as medium, and *magical or theological untranslatability*, 265–9.

Survivals of her early life: Algernon Blackwood, *The Centaur* (Harmondsworth: Penguin, 1938), 58–62; see also 107–8, 208, 259. As far as I can tell, *The Centaur* is currently out of print, except in print on demand editions, but it is readily available online. *Channel to the Earth's fair youth…Chiron*: 118–29. The frequency and interference of "mother" and "smother" connects *The Centaur* with the vocative Nature of the weird tale and its ambiguous guidance, whose roots are in the American wilderness. Nature's *mothering heart* may produce *smothered souls*: 249–50.

The rubric of the spectral: David Toop, *Sinister Resonance: The Mediumship of the Listener* (New York: Continuum, 2010), 125–78. On *preternatural hearing* in James Fenimore Cooper's wilderness novels, viii.

A distinct guidance: Blackwood, *The Centaur*, 58–62. On de-individuation and the herd, 198, 219, 262.

Geophony: Bernie Krause, *The Great Animal Orchestra: Finding the Origins of Music in the World's Wild Places* (London: Profile Books, 2012), 39.

The business of a writer: James Fenimore Cooper, *The Last of the Mohicans* (New York: Random House, 2005), xxxi.

In common with animal: Blackwood, *The Centaur*, 113. On what was common to the American Indian and the primordial Greek, as *old-world tribes and peoples with their babble of difficult tongues*, 166. On narrative form and destructuration, 37, 80, 107, 174, 192. *He remembered, for instance*: 223–4. The type scene with the sack of notebooks, 275. *The little poets*: 269–70. *Standing aloof*: 218 (my emphasis). *The litter of disordered notebooks*: 227. *At-one-ment*: 215. *Transition-blank*: 206. *The land toward which*: 106–7.

The idea of centaurs: Friedrich Hölderlin, *Poems and Fragments* (London: Anvil Press, 2004), 646–8.

Is it not a maimed and imperfect nature: Cited by Steve Nicholls, *Paradise Found: Nature in North America at the Time of Discovery* (Chicago: University of Chicago Press, 2009), 4.

Here, where the Argonauts once landed: Blackwood, *The Centaur*, 166. On the originary moment of Western sentimental consciousness, see Friedrich Schiller, *Essays* (New York: Continuum, 1998), 196.

By turns joyous: http://ghostbox.co.uk/artists-page/belbury-poly/

The realization of the vision of Caermaen: Arthur Machen, *The Great God Pan* and *The Hill of Dreams* (Mineola, NY: Dover Books, 2006), 112. On the magic of Hawthorne, 178–9. On the *wood whisper* and *mesh of the hills*: 170, 184, 196.

Dorcas, after the departure: Nathaniel Hawthorne, *Tales and Sketches* (New York: Library of America, 1997), 104–5.

Huge collective life…across the border: Algernon Blackwood, *Ancient Sorceries and Other Weird Stories* (London: Penguin, 2002), 227–31. The *wireless message from a vast Emitter*: 258. The *instinctive aversion she felt to being shut in*: 267.

Ring within ring…illegible hopeless scribblings: Machen, *The Hill of Dreams*, 233–5.

Wild beasts of the mountains: Homer, *Iliad*, Book 1, lines 266–8. *Father taught me how to travel*: Statius, *Achilleid*, Book 2, lines 96–166.

The concept of centaurs: Friedrich Hölderlin, *Poems and Fragments* (London: Anvil Press, 2004), 646–8. Translation by Google Translate.

To the Crow a horse is everything: Hank Real Bird in *Contrary Warriors: A Film of the Crow Tribe*, directed by Beth Ferris, Connie Poten, and Pamela Roberts (Los Angeles: Direct Cinema, 1986), 16-mm film. *I have been told*: Plenty-Coups in Frank Linderman, *Plenty-coups: Chief of the Crows* (Lincoln, NE: University of Nebraska Press, 2002), 55.

Centaur culture: N. Scott Momaday, *The Man Made of Words: Essays, Stories, Passages* (New York: St. Martin's Press, 1998), 165. *Edward Curtis preserved for us*: N. Scott Momaday in *Sacred Legacy: Edward S. Curtis and the North American Indian*, ed. Christopher Cardozo (New York: Simon & Schuster, 2000), 10.

The rays of Greek poetry…the sun sets: Henry David Thoreau, *A Week on the Concord and Merrimack Rivers* (New York: Library of America, 1985), 77.

3. Autarky and incoherent care

There was a lot of space: https://en.wikipedia.org/wiki/Martin_Hannett

There are no transcendental conditions: Gianni Vattimo and Pier Aldo Rovatti, *Weak Thought* (Albany, NY: State University of New York Press, 2012), 5.

Michelangelo Pistoletto's "Venus of the rags" can be seen here: http://www.tate.org.uk/art/artworks/pistoletto-venus-of-the-rags-t12200

On its *formal illumination*, see Germano Celant, *Arte Povera: History and Stories* (Milan: Electa, 2011) 156. According to Pistoletto, cited here by Celant, the rags "represent the confusion and multivalence of marginalized people," random and disparate communities that are the "rags" of society.

The stone that was alive: Giuseppe Penone in Celant, *Arte Povera*, 241. The work itself can be seen here:

http://www.nashersculpturecenter.org/art/exhibitions/exhibition?id=253

On Arte Povera and Italianness, see Celant, *Arte Povera*, 233, and Carolyn Christov-Bakargiev, *Arte Povera* (London: Phaidon, 1997), 28–46.

When I have set out: Jean-Jacques Rousseau, *Reveries of the Solitary Walker* (Harmondsworth: Penguin, 1979), 49.

Zero Books

CULTURE, SOCIETY & POLITICS

Contemporary culture has eliminated the concept and public figure of the intellectual. A cretinous anti-intellectualism presides, cheer-led by hacks in the pay of multinational corporations who reassure their bored readers that there is no need to rouse themselves from their stupor. Zer0 Books knows that another kind of discourse – intellectual without being academic, popular without being populist – is not only possible: it is already flourishing. Zer0 is convinced that in the unthinking, blandly consensual culture in which we live, critical and engaged theoretical reflection is more important than ever before.

If you have enjoyed this book, why not tell other readers by posting a review on your preferred book site.

Recent bestsellers from Zero Books are:

In the Dust of This Planet
Horror of Philosophy vol. 1
Eugene Thacker
In the first of a series of three books on the Horror of
Philosophy, *In the Dust of This Planet* offers the genre of horror
as a way of thinking about the unthinkable.
Paperback: 978-1-84694-676-9 ebook: 978-1-78099-010-1

Capitalist Realism
Is there no alternative?
Mark Fisher
An analysis of the ways in which capitalism has presented itself
as the only realistic political-economic system.
Paperback: 978-1-84694-317-1 ebook: 978-1-78099-734-6

Rebel Rebel
Chris O'Leary
David Bowie: every single song. Everything you want to know,
everything you didn't know.
Paperback: 978-1-78099-244-0 ebook: 978-1-78099-713-1

Cartographies of the Absolute
Alberto Toscano, Jeff Kinkle
An aesthetics of the economy for the twenty-first century.
Paperback: 978-1-78099-275-4 ebook: 978-1-78279-973-3

Malign Velocities
Accelerationism and Capitalism
Benjamin Noys
Long listed for the Bread and Roses Prize 2015, *Malign Velocities* argues against the need for speed, tracking acceleration as the symptom of the ongoing crises of capitalism.
Paperback: 978-1-78279-300-7 ebook: 978-1-78279-299-4

Meat Market
Female Flesh under Capitalism
Laurie Penny
A feminist dissection of women's bodies as the fleshy fulcrum of capitalist cannibalism, whereby women are both consumers and consumed.
Paperback: 978-1-84694-521-2 ebook: 978-1-84694-782-7

Poor but Sexy
Culture Clashes in Europe East and West
Agata Pyzik
How the East stayed East and the West stayed West.
Paperback: 978-1-78099-394-2 ebook: 978-1-78099-395-9

Romeo and Juliet in Palestine
Teaching Under Occupation
Tom Sperlinger
Life in the West Bank, the nature of pedagogy and the role of a university under occupation.
Paperback: 978-1-78279-637-4 ebook: 978-1-78279-636-7

Readers of ebooks can buy or view any of these bestsellers by clicking on the live link in the title. Most titles are published in paperback and as an ebook. Paperbacks are available in traditional bookshops. Both print and ebook formats are available online.

Find more titles and sign up to our readers' newsletter at http://www.johnhuntpublishing.com/culture-and-politics

Follow us on Facebook at https://www.facebook.com/ZeroBooks

and Twitter at https://twitter.com/Zer0Books